Doctor Who Astrology

Doctor Who Astrology

The Unofficial Astrological Guide

Matthew Petchinsky

Apophis Enterprises LLC

Doctor Who: Astrology: An Unofficial Astrology Guide
By Matthew Petchinsky

Message from the Author

Hello, Reader!

I know this has been a long time coming in the 60 years *Doctor Who* has been around. A Fan made book incorporating your first twelve Doctors. Yes, I did say 12, because of the 12 Zodiacs, I must apologize in advance for not having Doctors 13 to 15 in here.

I love the Show *Doctor Who*, I first got into the show when I was a kid, discovering it on *Scifi* channel (Before it was changed to '*Syfy*'). I have been watching the *Classic Doctor Who* on *Tubi*. I have been catching up with the newer Doctors with the dvds I received for Christmas, and have watch multiple times the *Doctor Who* on *Disney+*.

I hope you enjoy this book, as well as my 27 other books that you can find on *Amazon*, I have a lot more Hemp Astrology books coming out as well as a couple more Fiction books and the Second book of The Life and Banishment of Apophis: Book 2.

Let's begin.

Disclaimer

Disclaimer for "Doctor Who Astrology":

This work, "Doctor Who Astrology," is an independent, fan-made publication and is not authorized, approved, licensed, or endorsed by the creators or rights holders of "Doctor Who." The content within this book is created out of appreciation for the "Doctor Who" universe and is not intended for commercial use or profit. All references to "Doctor Who" within this publication are for the purpose of critique, review, and fan-based creativity only.

I, the author, claim no ownership over the trademarked name "Doctor Who," its characters, settings, or storylines, which remain the intellectual property of their respective copyright holders. This work is intended to be a tribute from a fan and is not plagiarized from any source material. It is an original creation inspired by the "Doctor Who" series, designed to offer a unique perspective and experience for fellow fans.

Any and all use of the "Doctor Who" name and related materials within this fan publication is done so under fair use for non-commercial, fan-based expression only. This disclaimer is to affirm that the creation of "Doctor Who Astrology" is done out of respect for the original work and its community of fans, and not for any personal gain.

Introduction to "Doctor Who Astrology"

At the heart of our boundless cosmos, amidst the swirling nebulas and the dancing constellations, lies an impending celestial event of unparalleled magnitude. This event, a cosmic alignment so rare and so powerful, threatens to unravel the very fabric of time and space, setting into motion a chain of events that could lead to the unravelling of reality as we know it. It is a moment poised on the brink of eternity, where the past, present, and future converge in a symphony of cosmic synchronicity. This is the universe on the cusp of change, a universe that calls out for a guardian. It calls out for the Doctor.

The Doctor, a timeless traveller in the vast expanse of the universe, has faced countless challenges, battled innumerable foes, and saved worlds beyond counting. Yet, the threat posed by this cosmic alignment is unlike any other. To navigate the complexities of this celestial puzzle, the Doctor must embark on a journey unlike any before - a journey through the essence of time itself, interacting with past and future incarnations, each embodying the characteristics and wisdom of the zodiac signs. This quest is not just a battle against time but a journey into the soul of the Doctor, exploring the depths of their being through the lens of astrology.

Astrology, the ancient practice of divining meaning and guidance through the positions of stars and planets, serves as the thematic backbone of "Doctor Who Astrology." It is a language that speaks of potential and possibility, of challenges and strengths, weaving the essence of each zodiac sign into the fabric of the Doctor's incarnations. Each sign, with its unique attributes and energies, mirrors the multifaceted nature of the Doctor, offering new insights into their character and choices. From the pioneering spirit of Aries to the compassionate depths of Pisces, every sign presents a world of exploration, setting the thematic tone for each Doctor's story within this cosmic adventure.

The significance of astrology in this narrative is not just a framework for exploration but a means to deepen our understanding of the

Doctor's character. It provides a lens through which we can explore the complexities of identity, fate, and free will. How does the fiery determination of a Leo manifest in the Doctor's actions? In what ways does the analytical mind of a Virgo influence their problem-solving strategies? "Doctor Who Astrology" invites readers to delve into these questions, embarking on a journey that is as much about the stars in the sky as it is about the stars within us.

As we stand on the brink of this cosmic alignment, "Doctor Who Astrology" promises a journey through time and space that is both a reflection and a discovery. It is a tale of adventure, of self-exploration, and of the unbreakable bonds that tie us to the universe. Welcome to a world where astrology and time travel intertwine, where the fate of the cosmos rests in the hands of the Doctor, guided by the stars themselves.

Chapter 1: Aries - The First Doctor (Warrior and Pioneer)

In the vast, ever-expanding canvas of the universe, where stars are born and galaxies dance in the eternal night, there emerges a tale of courage and initiation. This is the story of the First Doctor, an embodiment of Aries, the sign of the warrior and the pioneer. Known for his boldness, his pioneering spirit, and his unwavering courage, the First Doctor finds himself on the planet Varosha, a world under the iron grip of a tyrannical alien force known as the Kaldorans.

The Kaldorans, with their advanced technology and merciless rule, have enslaved the inhabitants of Varosha, bending the planet to their will. The once vibrant world, known across the stars for its lush landscapes and the indomitable spirit of its people, now lies shrouded in despair. But in the heart of this darkness, a spark of rebellion flickers, awaiting the gust that will ignite it into a blaze. That gust comes in the form of the Doctor.

Landing on Varosha in his TARDIS, disguised as an inconspicuous piece of ancient ruins, the First Doctor steps out into a world crying out for change. With his keen sense of justice and an innate desire to right wrongs, he quickly discerns the plight of the Varoshans. The Doctor's arrival does not go unnoticed. Among the shadows of the oppressed, whispers of a stranger who has the power to challenge the Kaldorans begin to spread. It is in these whispers that the Doctor sees the opportunity to spark the rebellion Varosha needs.

Embodying the characteristics of Aries, the First Doctor takes to this challenge with a headstrong determination. Aries, ruled by Mars, the planet of war and energy, imbues the Doctor with a warrior's spirit and a leader's resolve. He knows that to inspire the Varoshans to rise against their oppressors, he must embody the very essence of rebellion. Thus, he begins to sow the seeds of dissent, using his intelligence and strategic mind to outwit the Kaldorans at every turn.

The Doctor's first act of rebellion comes in the form of sabotage. He infiltrates the Kaldorans' command center, a towering fortress that looms over the main settlement, a symbol of their dominance. Here, he employs his vast knowledge of technology to disrupt the Kaldorans' control mechanisms, causing chaos within their ranks and giving the Varoshans their first taste of hope.

But true to the nature of Aries, the Doctor does not stop at clandestine sabotage. He takes to the streets, rallying the Varoshans with impassioned speeches that ignite the fire of rebellion in their hearts. He speaks of freedom, of the right to determine one's own destiny, and of the strength that lies in unity. His words, powerful and raw, resonate with the Varoshans, who see in him not just a leader, but a symbol of their potential liberation.

As the rebellion gains momentum, the Doctor leads from the front, embodying Aries' boldness. He does not shy away from confrontation, facing the Kaldorans' might with a courage that inspires his followers. The battles are fierce, and the cost is high, but under the Doctor's leadership, the Varoshans begin to reclaim their world.

The climax of this rebellion comes with a daring assault on the Kaldorans' stronghold. The Doctor, leveraging his strategic genius, orchestrates a plan that utilizes the unique geography of Varosha to the rebels' advantage. It is a battle that will be remembered in Varoshan history, not just for its boldness, but for the spirit of freedom that it represents.

In the aftermath of the rebellion, as peace begins to return to Varosha, the Doctor, ever the wanderer, knows that his time on this world has come to an end. He leaves behind a liberated planet, a people once again in control of their destiny, and a legacy of courage and determination.

The First Doctor, as Aries, begins the cosmic journey of "Doctor Who Astrology" not just as a warrior and a pioneer, but as a beacon of hope in the fight against oppression. His story is a testament to the power of courage, leadership, and the pioneering spirit that drives us to reach beyond our limits, challenging us to fight for what is right, no matter the odds.

Chapter 2: Taurus - The Second Doctor (The Stable Force)

In the ceaseless voyage through the cosmos, where the fabric of reality weaves and unwinds in the hands of time itself, there lies a planet unlike any other. This world, known as Ephemera, is a place where reality shifts as unpredictably as the winds, challenging the very notion of stability and constancy. It is here that the Second Doctor, an embodiment of Taurus, the steadfast and resilient bull, makes his entrance. Reflecting Taurus' traits of determination, patience, and an unshakeable connection to the tangible world, the Second Doctor confronts Ephemera's challenges with a calm and enduring spirit.

The planet Ephemera, with its ever-changing landscapes and shifting terrains, presents a unique challenge. Reality on Ephemera is in a constant state of flux, with mountains dissolving into rivers and forests turning into deserts in the blink of an eye. For its inhabitants, life is a perpetual adaptation, a never-ending struggle to find stability in chaos. It is a world that cries out for the grounding presence of Taurus, and the Second Doctor answers that call.

Landing on Ephemera with his companions, the Doctor is immediately confronted with the planet's unpredictable nature. Their initial explorations lead them through landscapes that shift under their feet, forcing them to rely on the Doctor's unflappable nature. The Second Doctor, much like Taurus, draws upon his inner reservoir of resilience and determination, traits bestowed upon him by his zodiac sign, ruled by Venus, the planet of love and beauty. This connection to Venus imbues the Doctor with a deep appreciation for the physical world, an appreciation that becomes his guiding light on Ephemera.

The trials faced by the Doctor and his companions on Ephemera are not merely physical but emotional and psychological. The shifting reality tests their perceptions and their faith in the tangible. Here, the

Doctor's Taurean qualities shine brightest. His steadfast nature, his patience, and his ability to remain grounded in the face of the incomprehensible become the cornerstone of their survival.

As the Doctor navigates the challenges of Ephemera, he discovers the source of the planet's instability: a malfunctioning reality engine, a remnant of a bygone civilization that sought to control the very fabric of existence. The engine, damaged and forgotten, has been warping the reality of Ephemera for centuries, creating a world where nothing remains constant.

Understanding the nature of the problem, the Doctor sets about repairing the reality engine. His approach is methodical, patient, and unwavering, embodying the earthy stability of Taurus. This task requires not just technical expertise but a deep understanding of the physical laws that govern the universe, an understanding rooted in the Doctor's appreciation for the material world.

With his companions by his side, the Doctor works tirelessly to stabilize the reality engine. It is a task that demands patience, for the engine is complex and the solutions are not immediately apparent. Yet, the Doctor's determination never wanes. His Taurean resilience shines as a beacon of hope in the unpredictable world of Ephemera.

Finally, after what seems like an eternity, the reality engine is stabilized. The landscapes of Ephemera cease their chaotic shifting, and for the first time in centuries, the planet knows stability. The Doctor, with his earthy pragmatism and steadfast resolve, has restored balance to a world torn by constant change.

As the Second Doctor prepares to leave Ephemera, his impact is evident not just in the stabilized landscapes but in the hearts of its people. He has taught them the value of perseverance, the strength that lies in patience, and the beauty of a stable reality. His departure is marked by a newfound sense of peace on Ephemera, a testament to the stabilizing force of Taurus.

Chapter 2 of "Doctor Who Astrology," featuring the Second Doctor as Taurus, is not just a story of overcoming environmental challenges but a narrative that highlights the importance of stability, resilience, and determination. The Second Doctor, as the embodiment of Taurus, leaves behind a legacy of earthy stability, demonstrating that even in a universe of infinite possibilities, the strength of the steady and the patient can prevail.

Chapter 3: Gemini - The Third Doctor (The Communicator)

In the intricate tapestry of the cosmos, where stars whisper secrets to the void, and planets dance in silent harmony, communication becomes the thread that binds the universe together. On the planet of Serenia, a jewel suspended in the dark velvet of space, this thread is stretched thin to the brink of breaking. Two ancient and powerful races, the Selenians and the Dorianites, stand on the precipice of war, their once-peaceful coexistence shattered by misunderstandings and mistrust. It is into this precarious situation that the Third Doctor, an embodiment of Gemini, the sign of the Twins, is drawn, tasked with the monumental challenge of averting a conflict that threatens to engulf the planet.

The Third Doctor, mirroring Gemini's adaptability, intellect, and exceptional communication skills, finds himself navigating a complex web of political intrigue and deep-seated prejudice. Gemini, ruled by Mercury, the planet of communication, grants the Doctor an unparalleled ability to understand and adapt to both sides of the conflict. His approach is not one of brute force but of diplomacy and dialogue, recognizing that the key to resolving the crisis lies in bridging the chasm of misunderstanding between the Selenians and the Dorianites.

As the Doctor delves deeper into the heart of the conflict, he discovers a series of sabotages and false flags, each designed to stoke the fires of animosity between the two races. It becomes apparent that there are those who seek to benefit from the war, shadowy figures who lurk behind the scenes, manipulating events to their own dark ends. With the stakes higher than ever, the Doctor's Gemini traits of quick thinking and adaptability become his greatest assets.

Employing his sharp wit and vast intellect, the Doctor embarks on a dual mission: to expose the conspirators behind the sabotage and to facilitate a dialogue between the Selenians and the Dorianites. His efforts lead him to a series of clandestine meetings, dangerous investigations, and high-stakes negotiations. Each step of the way, the Doctor exemplifies the Gemini qualities of versatility and mental agility, navigating the complex socio-political landscape of Serenia with ease.

One of the Doctor's most significant challenges comes in the form of a peace summit, where leaders of the Selenians and the Dorianites come together for the first time in decades. The atmosphere is tense, charged with the weight of centuries of history and the potential for future conflict. Here, the Doctor's communicative prowess shines. He crafts his words with the precision of a poet and the clarity of a diplomat, weaving together arguments and perspectives that highlight the common ground between the two races. His speeches are not just appeals to reason but to the shared values and aspirations that bind all sentient beings.

The Doctor's efforts to foster understanding and empathy between the Selenians and the Dorianites are not without their challenges. Missteps are made, and tempers flare, threatening to derail the delicate process of reconciliation. Yet, the Doctor remains undeterred, his Gemini resilience and adaptability allowing him to navigate these setbacks with grace and ingenuity.

In the end, the Doctor's strategy begins to bear fruit. The revelation of the true architects behind the conflict, coupled with the Doctor's tireless efforts to facilitate dialogue, leads to a breakthrough. The Selenians and the Dorianites start to see beyond their differences, recognizing the futility of war and the value of peace.

As the Third Doctor prepares to leave Serenia, the planet stands on the dawn of a new era, one of peace and cooperation. His role as the communicator, the bridge between worlds and hearts, has averted a catastrophic war and laid the foundation for lasting harmony.

Chapter 3 of "Doctor Who Astrology," with the Third Doctor as Gemini, is a testament to the power of communication, adaptability, and intellect. It underscores the idea that in the vast and varied universe, the ability to understand and to be understood is perhaps the most powerful force of all. The Third Doctor, through his Gemini essence, embodies this force, proving that even in the face of imminent conflict, words can heal, connect, and create new beginnings.

Chapter 4: Cancer - The Fourth Doctor (The Guardian)

Amidst the sprawling expanse of the cosmos, where the fabric of space-time weaves the destiny of countless civilizations, there exists a planet teetering on the brink of monumental discovery. This world, named Zephyria, is home to a race of beings at the cusp of unlocking the secrets of interstellar travel, a breakthrough that promises to catapult their society into a new era of exploration and enlightenment. However, with great discovery comes great vulnerability. The Zephyrians, in their innocence and thirst for knowledge, unknowingly stand on the precipice of danger, drawing the covetous gaze of intergalactic marauders who prey upon such emerging civilizations. It is against this backdrop of potential and peril that the Fourth Doctor, embodying the nurturing and protective essence of Cancer, arrives to serve as their guardian.

The Fourth Doctor, with his characteristic flourish of his scarf and an ever-present twinkle of wisdom in his eyes, quickly perceives the delicate balance of the situation. Cancer, his guiding sign, ruled by the Moon, imparts to him an unparalleled depth of empathy and an intuitive understanding of the emotional and psychological landscapes of those he aims to protect. Zephyria, with its vibrant culture and earnest ambitions, resonates deeply with the Doctor's Cancerian essence, compelling him to shield this nascent civilization from the shadows that seek to exploit it.

The Doctor's approach is not one of overt confrontation but of subtle guidance and emotional support. He embeds himself within Zephyrian society, offering his vast knowledge as a resource while fostering a space for the Zephyrians to express their hopes, fears, and dreams. His ability to listen and genuinely connect with the Zephyrians strengthens their resolve and unity, qualities essential for the challenges ahead.

As the Doctor delves deeper into the fabric of Zephyrian society, he uncovers the looming threat of the marauders, a ruthless coalition of species known for their technological prowess and moral bankruptcy.

They aim to enslave the Zephyrians, turning their breakthrough against them, converting a dawn of exploration into an era of subjugation. The Doctor's protective instincts, fueled by his Cancerian nature, surge to the forefront. He knows that the key to safeguarding Zephyria lies not in weaponry or warfare but in the hearts and minds of its people.

Employing his deep empathetic connection and understanding of emotional depths, the Doctor begins to fortify Zephyria from within. He initiates a cultural renaissance, emphasizing the strength found in communal bonds and shared dreams. Through tales of other worlds and civilizations, some thriving in harmony, others cautionary tales of division leading to downfall, the Doctor weaves a narrative that unites the Zephyrians like never before. Their newfound unity becomes their shield, a protective barrier no marauder can penetrate.

However, the Doctor knows that true protection involves preparation for self-sufficiency. He gently guides the Zephyrians in developing their technology in a manner that emphasizes defense and self-reliance. Under his tutelage, they learn to shield their planet from external threats and to navigate the stars with a philosophy of peace and exploration. The Doctor's intuitive understanding of timing and his ability to foresee potential outcomes shape these teachings, ensuring that Zephyria's entry into the galactic community is marked by wisdom and respect.

In the climax of this chapter, as the marauders make their inevitable approach, they find not a vulnerable civilization ripe for conquest but a united, resilient society. Their attempts at invasion are thwarted not by force but by the indomitable spirit of a people empowered by knowledge and bound by a shared vision of their future. The Doctor, watching from the sidelines, allows the Zephyrians to stand in their own light, his role as the guardian fulfilled not by making them dependent on him but by enabling them to protect themselves.

As the Fourth Doctor takes his leave, Zephyria shines brighter than before, a beacon of hope and a testament to the strength found in nurturing, protection, and intuitive understanding. His departure is bittersweet, but the legacy he leaves behind is immeasurable. Chapter

4 of "Doctor Who Astrology," with the Fourth Doctor as Cancer, encapsulates the profound impact of empathy, protection, and the deep emotional connections that bind us all, reminding us that the greatest strength often lies in the gentlest touch.

Chapter 5: Leo - The Fifth Doctor (The Hero)

In a distant sector of the galaxy, where tradition clashes with the thirst for spectacle, lies the planet Meridia. Meridia is a world where honor and valor are prized above all, and its citizens are the avid spectators of a gladiatorial contest known as the Solar Games. These games are not mere sport but a testament to the Meridian ideals of strength, courage, and leadership. It is into this arena of valor that the Fifth Doctor, embodying the fiery spirit and natural heroism of Leo, is drawn, not by choice but by the machinations of fate that threaten his companions.

The Fifth Doctor, with his cricket blazer and a stalk of celery adorning his lapel, might seem an unlikely candidate for the brutal Solar Games. Yet, within him burns the heart of a Leo, a sign ruled by the Sun, symbolizing warmth, generosity, and a courage that can outshine the darkness of the most dire situations. His arrival on Meridia coincides with a critical juncture in the planet's history, where the integrity of the Solar Games is under threat from corruption that seeks to transform the honorable contest into a spectacle of savagery for entertainment.

The Doctor's companions, having been mistaken for participants in a nefarious plot to undermine the Solar Games, are held captive, their fates tied to the outcome of the games. It becomes immediately clear to the Doctor that the only way to save them is to enter the arena himself, not as a doctor, but as a gladiator. Embracing the Leo archetype, he steps into the role with a bravery that inspires both allies and rivals alike.

The games are a trial by fire, a series of challenges that test not just physical prowess but the spirit of leadership and the capacity for self-sacrifice. Each trial is designed to push the contestants to their limits, yet in every challenge, the Doctor's Leonine qualities shine through. His leadership galvanizes the other gladiators, his warmth and generosity earning their loyalty and friendship, turning potential rivals into allies. His bravery becomes a beacon, illuminating the path to not just survival, but honor.

Amidst the trials, the Doctor uncovers a deeper malaise afflicting Meridia, a rot within that threatens the very essence of what the Solar Games stand for. A shadowy coalition of power brokers, betting on the outcomes and reveling in the spectacle of violence, seeks to manipulate the games for their own gain. The Doctor's heroism thus finds a dual purpose: to save his companions and to restore the honor of the Solar Games.

With the sun of Meridia high in the sky, casting its golden light upon the arena, the Doctor faces his final challenge. It is a spectacle that draws the eyes of all Meridia, a battle not just of strength but of ideals. In this climactic moment, the Doctor's strategy, charisma, and courage converge. He outwits and outplays the corrupt forces seeking to control the games, exposing their machinations to the public gaze, and in doing so, he rekindles the true spirit of the Solar Games among the citizens of Meridia.

The resolution of the games sees the Doctor's companions freed and the honor of the Solar Games restored. The Doctor, with his Leonine heart, has not only saved his friends but has also ignited a revolution in Meridia, a return to the values of honor, valor, and integrity. His departure from Meridia is marked by a celebration in his honor, a testament to the warmth and heroism he brought to a world on the brink of losing its way.

Chapter 5 of "Doctor Who Astrology," featuring the Fifth Doctor as Leo, is a tale of heroism that burns bright in the face of adversity. It is a story that celebrates the qualities of leadership, bravery, and warmth that define Leo, showcasing how, even in the darkest of arenas, the light of a hero can shine the way to redemption and honor. The Doctor, as Leo, embodies the fiery spirit of a hero who rises to the occasion, not for glory, but for the sake of those he seeks to protect, leaving behind a legacy that will burn bright in the annals of Meridia's history.

Chapter 6: Virgo - The Sixth Doctor (The Analyst)

In the labyrinthine corridors of the cosmos, where reality bends and logic twists into enigma, there exists a universe unlike any other. This universe, known to the few who have glimpsed its complexities as the Puzzle-Box Universe, is a realm where causality loops and paradoxes are the fabric of existence, a creation of an advanced civilization that sought to challenge the bounds of intellect and understanding. It is into this intricate maze of mysteries that the Sixth Doctor, embodying the meticulous and intellectual essence of Virgo, finds himself drawn, a challenge that would demand the utmost of his analytical skills and attention to detail.

The Sixth Doctor, with his vibrant patchwork coat and an ever-present air of confidence, is no stranger to the peculiar and the paradoxical. However, the Puzzle-Box Universe presents a challenge of a different magnitude. Its very nature, a constantly evolving series of puzzles and traps designed to test and confound, resonates with the Virgoan qualities of analysis, discernment, and methodical approach. For the Doctor, the stakes are personal; trapped within the universe are his companions, ensnared by the latest iteration of puzzles that threaten to erase them from existence if not solved in time.

The Puzzle-Box Universe is a reflection of Virgo's symbol, the Virgin, representing purity of thought and precision. Each challenge the Doctor faces is layered with complexity, requiring not just intellectual prowess but a keen attention to detail and an unwavering patience. The puzzles range from spatial anomalies that distort perception to temporal riddles that twist time into impossible knots. Each solution brings the Doctor closer to his companions, but also deeper into the heart of the universe's greatest mystery: its purpose and creator.

With the analytical mind of Virgo guiding him, the Doctor begins to see patterns in the puzzles, a method to the madness. He approaches each challenge with a systematic precision, deconstructing the complexities with a calm that belies the urgency of his quest. His meticulous nature becomes his greatest asset, allowing him to navigate the treacherous reality of the Puzzle-Box Universe with a clarity that slowly unravels its secrets.

As the Doctor delves deeper into the universe, he uncovers the truth behind its creation. It was designed not as a trap, but as a test, a means to find an intellect capable of understanding the universe's creators and, ultimately, of making contact. The Doctor's journey through the puzzles is revealed to be a path towards a meeting of minds across the vast expanse of space and time, a dialogue with beings of immense knowledge and insight.

The final puzzle, the key to unlocking the universe and freeing his companions, challenges the Doctor to transcend the analytical and embrace a broader understanding of the universe. It is a test that calls upon not just his Virgoan traits but the entirety of his experience and wisdom. With a solution that is as much about intuition as it is about logic, the Doctor succeeds, bridging the gap between himself and the creators of the Puzzle-Box Universe.

In the aftermath of the resolution, as the Doctor and his companions stand on the threshold of returning to their own reality, the creators offer a parting gift. They share a glimpse of the cosmos through their eyes, an intricate tapestry of cause and effect, of chaos and order. It is a perspective that deepens the Doctor's already profound understanding of the universe, a reminder of the balance between analysis and intuition.

Chapter 6 of "Doctor Who Astrology," featuring the Sixth Doctor as Virgo, is a celebration of the analytical mind's power to solve, to understand, and ultimately, to connect. The Doctor, through his Virgoan essence, demonstrates that the path to understanding the universe's mysteries is not just through meticulous analysis but through recognizing the interconnectedness of all things. It is a tale that highlights the methodical approach and intellectual rigor of Virgo, embodied in a

Doctor who faces the complexities of existence with a keen mind and a detailed eye, forever seeking to unravel the puzzles of the cosmos.

Chapter 7: Libra - The Seventh Doctor (The Strategist)

In the grand theater of the cosmos, where the delicate dance of diplomacy and the sharp edges of conflict often intersect, there lies the planet of Paxos. Paxos, a world renowned for its beauty and diversity, has long been a meeting ground for civilizations seeking to resolve their differences through dialogue rather than war. It is here, against the backdrop of a peace conference that teeters on the brink of disaster, that the Seventh Doctor, embodying the equilibrium and fairness of Libra, takes the stage as the ultimate strategist.

The peace conference on Paxos is no ordinary gathering. It is a last-ditch effort to avert a galactic war, with delegates from the warring factions harboring centuries of animosity and mistrust. The tension in the air is palpable, each word and gesture carrying the weight of potential conflict. Into this volatile mix steps the Seventh Doctor, with his iconic question-mark umbrella and a keen understanding of the nuances of diplomacy. Libra, his guiding sign, lends him an innate sense of balance and justice, qualities that are sorely needed to navigate the intricate web of politics and relationships on display.

The Doctor's approach to the impending crisis is twofold: on one hand, he seeks to understand the root causes of the conflict, delving into the history and grievances of each faction with a meticulousness that belies his whimsical appearance. On the other, he works to build bridges, using his Libran charm and wit to soften hearts and open minds. His goal is not just to prevent war but to foster a lasting peace, one built on understanding and mutual respect.

As the conference progresses, the Doctor's diplomatic skills are put to the test. He faces a myriad of challenges, from hardline factions that see peace as a sign of weakness to external forces that seek to benefit from the continuation of conflict. Each obstacle requires a delicate balancing act, a combination of firm resolve and diplomatic finesse that only a Libran could manage.

One of the turning points in the conference comes when the Doctor orchestrates a series of private meetings between the leaders of the warring factions. These meetings, held in secret and away from the prying eyes of the media and hardliners, allow for a frank and open exchange of views. The Doctor, acting as mediator, uses his strategic mind to guide the conversation, highlighting common ground and gently challenging the leaders to see beyond their immediate grievances.

The Doctor's strategy also involves a more unconventional approach. Recognizing that the conflict's roots lie deep in the past, he uses his knowledge of time travel to offer the leaders a glimpse of their potential future, one shaped by the outcome of the conference. This vision of what could be, both the promise of peace and the threat of continued war, serves as a powerful motivator, compelling the leaders to consider the legacy they wish to leave behind.

As the conference reaches its climax, the Doctor's efforts begin to bear fruit. The atmosphere of animosity and suspicion gives way to cautious optimism. Agreements are reached, not just on the cessation of hostilities but on the framework for a lasting peace. The Doctor's role as the Libran strategist, balancing the scales of justice and diplomacy, proves instrumental in guiding the delegates from the brink of disaster to the dawn of a new era of cooperation.

Chapter 7 of "Doctor Who Astrology," featuring the Seventh Doctor as Libra, is a testament to the power of diplomacy and strategic thinking. The Doctor, through his embodiment of Libra's qualities, demonstrates that even in the face of overwhelming odds, balance can be restored, and peace achieved. It is a chapter that highlights the importance of fairness, strategy, and the delicate art of mediation, reminding us that in the grand scheme of the cosmos, balance is not just a concept but a practice, a path to a brighter, more harmonious future.

Chapter 8: Scorpio - The Eighth Doctor (The Transformer)

In the uncharted depths of the universe, where darkness holds dominion and the stars whisper secrets of ancient times, a cosmic entity known as the Void Weaver weaves its insidious tapestry. This entity, older than time itself, seeks not dominion or destruction but the erasure of histories, the obliteration of the narratives that give meaning to existence. Into this shadowy theatre steps the Eighth Doctor, embodying the intense and transformative power of Scorpio, to confront a threat that challenges not only the fabric of the universe but the very essence of identity.

The Eighth Doctor, with his Victorian elegance and eyes that seem to hold centuries of secrets, is uniquely suited to this challenge. Scorpio, his guiding sign, is associated with themes of death and rebirth, of delving into the depths to confront the darkness and emerge transformed. The Void Weaver's threat, then, is not just a cosmic challenge but a deeply personal one, inviting the Doctor into a dance with the shadows that lurk within the universe and within himself.

The Doctor's journey to confront the Void Weaver takes him through realms that test the limits of his understanding and courage. He traverses the Forgotten Zones, places wiped clean by the Void Weaver, where echoes of lost civilizations whisper their despair. Here, the Doctor is confronted with the raw pain of erasure, the agony of worlds and peoples who have been unmade. It is a journey that forces him to confront the impermanence of existence, a stark reflection of Scorpio's themes of death and transformation.

But it is not just the universe's dark corners that the Doctor must navigate; he must also delve into the darker parts of his own psyche. Scorpio's influence brings to the fore the Doctor's own fears and doubts, his internal conflicts, and the parts of himself that he has long kept hidden. This introspective journey is as challenging as the external one, for the Doctor must confront the possibility of his own histories being unwoven, his own existence being rendered a void.

The confrontation with the Void Weaver, when it comes, is a battle of wits and wills. The entity, a being of pure energy and consciousness, seeks to unmake the Doctor as it has unmade countless others. But the Doctor, armed with the depth and intensity of Scorpio, turns the battle into one of transformation. He engages the Void Weaver not with weapons but with the power of narrative, of stories that hold the essence of the worlds it has sought to erase.

In a climactic moment of unity between the Doctor and the lost echoes of the Forgotten Zones, a new narrative is woven, one that incorporates the Void Weaver's darkness into a story of rebirth and renewal. This act of transformation, of taking the raw material of pain and loss and weaving it into something new, something meaningful, is the essence of Scorpio's power.

As the Void Weaver is subdued, its power to erase histories neutralized, the universe begins the slow process of remembering the unmade worlds. The Doctor, too, emerges from the confrontation transformed. He carries with him the depth of the experiences, the knowledge that even in the face of the greatest darkness, transformation and rebirth are possible.

Chapter 8 of "Doctor Who Astrology," featuring the Eighth Doctor as Scorpio, is a journey into the heart of darkness, both cosmic and personal. It explores the themes of death, rebirth, and the transformative power of confronting the shadowy parts of the universe and oneself. The Eighth Doctor, with Scorpio's intensity and depth, demonstrates that even in the deepest darkness, there is the potential for light, for change, and for profound transformation. This chapter is a testament to the enduring power of stories, the narratives that define us, and the unbreakable thread of hope that runs through the tapestry of existence.

Chapter 9: Sagittarius - The Ninth Doctor (The Explorer)

In the sprawling, infinite expanse of the cosmos, where the stars are beacons of mysteries waiting to be unraveled, the Ninth Doctor emerges as the quintessential explorer, propelled by the fiery spirit and boundless curiosity of Sagittarius. His era is marked by a relentless pursuit of freedom, a journey across the stars that embodies the archer's love for exploration and the thirst for knowledge that lies beyond the known boundaries of time and space. It is during one of these voyages that the Ninth Doctor stumbles upon a mystery that spans the galaxy, a puzzle so intricate that it challenges his understanding of the universe and his place within it.

The mystery at the heart of this adventure is a signal, ancient and enigmatic, emanating from the forgotten corners of the galaxy. This signal, imbued with a strange energy, has the power to bend reality, creating rifts where the past and the future collide in unpredictable ways. The Doctor, with his innate Sagittarian optimism and philosophical nature, is drawn to this phenomenon, seeing in it not just a challenge, but an opportunity to explore the very fabric of existence.

The Ninth Doctor's journey to unravel the mystery of the signal takes him to worlds that defy imagination. He navigates the ruins of civilizations that have risen and fallen in the wake of the signal's power, each world offering a piece of the puzzle and a reflection on the nature of freedom and destiny. These explorations are not without their dangers, for the signal attracts those who seek to harness its power for their own ends. Yet, the Doctor's Sagittarian spirit, his unwavering belief in the goodness of the universe and the value of every life, guides him through these challenges.

As the Doctor delves deeper into the mystery, his optimistic and philosophical nature comes to the fore. He engages with beings who have been touched by the signal, listening to their stories and learning from their experiences. These interactions, marked by the Doctor's genuine curiosity and empathy, reveal the dual nature of the signal: it is both a harbinger of chaos and a catalyst for change, a force that can unravel the fabric of reality or weave it into something new.

The climax of the Doctor's quest brings him face to face with the source of the signal: an ancient artifact, a relic of a civilization that sought to understand the fundamental forces of the universe. The artifact, damaged and forgotten, has been broadcasting the signal across the ages, calling out for someone who could repair it, someone who could understand its purpose. The Doctor, with his Sagittarian blend of wisdom and wanderlust, is that someone.

In repairing the artifact, the Doctor not only ends the threat posed by the signal but also unlocks the secrets it held. He discovers that the artifact was a tool for exploration, a means to traverse the universe in a way that transcended physical travel. It was a gift from a civilization that valued freedom and knowledge above all, a civilization that, in many ways, reflected the Doctor's own Sagittarian ideals.

The resolution of the mystery leaves the universe a little safer, a little more understood. But for the Ninth Doctor, the journey is far from over. With the artifact repaired and the knowledge it contains added to his own, he sets off once again, his spirit unbound, his heart aflame with the desire to explore, to learn, and to experience the endless wonder of the cosmos.

Chapter 9 of "Doctor Who Astrology," featuring the Ninth Doctor as Sagittarius, is a testament to the power of exploration, both external and internal. It celebrates the Sagittarian qualities of optimism, philosophical depth, and the relentless pursuit of freedom and knowledge. The Ninth Doctor, as the explorer, reminds us that the universe is not just a place of darkness and danger, but also of light, of mystery, and of boundless potential waiting to be discovered.

Chapter 10: Capricorn - The Tenth Doctor (The Achiever)

In the vast, cold expanse of the universe, where the light of distant stars struggles to pierce the darkness, a crisis of cosmic proportions brews. A galaxy teeters on the brink of annihilation, threatened by an ancient force known only as The Darkness. It consumes stars, planets, and life, leaving behind nothing but the void. Into this dire situation steps the Tenth Doctor, the embodiment of Capricorn's ambition, determination, and practicality, poised to confront a challenge that would test the limits of his resolve and leadership.

The Tenth Doctor, with his sharp suit, manic energy, and an ever-ready wit, may seem an unlikely figure to embody the stoic and disciplined nature of Capricorn. Yet, beneath his charismatic exterior lies a core of steel, a resolve forged in the fires of countless battles and losses. It is this resolve, this unyielding dedication to the greater good, that marks him as the Achiever among the stars.

The challenge presented by The Darkness is not just one of strength but of strategy and endurance. It is a force that cannot be defeated by conventional means; its very nature defies the physics and logic upon which much of the Doctor's actions are based. Facing such an adversary requires not just power but a plan, a methodical approach that can only be driven by Capricorn's disciplined nature.

The Doctor's strategy unfolds in stages, each step a testament to his practical approach and deep understanding of the universe's laws. First, he seeks to understand The Darkness, delving into ancient texts and forgotten lore, consulting with beings who have existed since the dawn of time. This quest for knowledge is driven by Capricorn's need for mastery, the ambition to overcome through understanding.

With knowledge in hand, the Doctor begins the task of rallying allies, drawing together a coalition of civilizations that The Darkness threatens. This endeavor highlights another facet of Capricorn's nature: leadership. The Doctor's leadership, however, is not born of charisma alone but of the respect he commands through his actions, his history of sacrifices, and his unwavering commitment to the cause.

The final plan to confront The Darkness is a masterpiece of tactical ingenuity, requiring precise coordination across the galaxy, the harnessing of energies and technologies beyond the comprehension of many. Yet, it is the Doctor's practicality, his ability to distill complex concepts into actionable plans, that makes the impossible possible. His dedication, a hallmark of Capricorn, shines brightest in these moments, driving him to push himself and his allies to the limits of their abilities.

As the confrontation with The Darkness unfolds, the Doctor's resolve is tested as never before. The battle is grueling, a war of attrition against a seemingly unstoppable force. Yet, even in the face of overwhelming odds, the Doctor's discipline and determination do not waver. Capricorn's influence ensures that he remains focused, utilizing every resource, every ally, every ounce of knowledge to push back The Darkness.

The victory, when it comes, is not without cost. The galaxy is saved, but the scars of the battle are deep, both on the canvas of the cosmos and in the Doctor's heart. Yet, even in the aftermath, the Doctor's Capricornian nature is evident. He takes responsibility for the reconstruction efforts, his practical approach guiding the healing process, his leadership inspiring those around him to rebuild better, stronger.

Chapter 10 of "Doctor Who Astrology," featuring the Tenth Doctor as Capricorn, is a narrative of ambition, discipline, and determination. It showcases the Capricornian traits of practicality and unwavering dedication, illustrating how these qualities can save an entire galaxy. The Tenth Doctor, as the Achiever, reminds us that even in the face of the abyss, the discipline to plan, the resolve to act, and the ambition to strive for the greater good can illuminate the darkest of times.

Chapter 11: Aquarius - The Eleventh Doctor (The Innovator)

In the far reaches of the future, within a society that prides itself on its technological advancements and harmonious existence, a hidden discord festers. This world, Utopia Prime, stands as a beacon of progress, yet beneath its polished surface lies a rigid adherence to outdated ideologies that stifle true innovation and equality. It is into this paradoxical paradise that the Eleventh Doctor, a living embodiment of Aquarius' spirit of originality and humanitarianism, arrives. His mission: to usher in a new era of enlightenment by challenging the status quo and introducing revolutionary ideas.

The Eleventh Doctor, with his quirky bow tie and an endless sense of wonder, personifies Aquarius' forward-thinking nature and its detachment from conventions. His arrival in Utopia Prime is met with curiosity and suspicion in equal measure. The society's governing council, the Custodians, is particularly wary of the Doctor's influence, fearing that his radical ideas could undermine their control.

However, the Doctor's interest lies not in power plays but in the betterment of society. He quickly identifies the core issues stifling Utopia Prime: a lack of creativity in solving social problems, an overreliance on technology that has led to a disconnect from nature, and a societal structure that prioritizes conformity over individual expression. These challenges resonate deeply with the Doctor's Aquarian ideals, inspiring him to act as a catalyst for change.

The Doctor begins his quest for societal transformation by engaging with the citizens of Utopia Prime, from the intellectuals and artists to the workers and outcasts. His approach is unconventional, leveraging his vast knowledge and experience to spark discussions and debates that encourage people to think beyond their current reality. He organizes symposiums, interactive workshops, and public demonstrations that showcase the power of innovative thinking and the potential for technology to serve humanity in more holistic ways.

One of the Doctor's most radical proposals is the creation of "Idea Incubators," spaces where individuals from all walks of life can come together to share ideas, collaborate on projects, and experiment with new technologies. These incubators become hotbeds of creativity and innovation, leading to breakthroughs in sustainable energy, environmental restoration, and social equality.

As these revolutionary ideas begin to take root, the Custodians attempt to clamp down, fearing the loss of their control. However, the tide of change is too strong to be halted. The Doctor, leveraging his Aquarian knack for strategy and his ability to inspire and mobilize, orchestrates a series of events that demonstrate the positive impacts of the new approaches on society.

The climax of the Doctor's quest comes when he facilitates a groundbreaking dialogue between the Custodians and a coalition of Utopia Prime's citizens. Through a series of negotiations, characterized by the Doctor's insightful mediation and Aquarius-inspired idealism, a new governance model is agreed upon. This model is based on inclusivity, collective decision-making, and the prioritization of innovation for the common good.

As the Doctor prepares to leave Utopia Prime, the society stands on the brink of a new dawn. The changes he has initiated have sparked a renaissance of thought and innovation, setting the planet on a path toward a truly utopian future. The Eleventh Doctor's legacy is one of transformation, a testament to the power of Aquarius' forward-thinking nature and its commitment to humanitarian ideals.

Chapter 11 of "Doctor Who Astrology," featuring the Eleventh Doctor as Aquarius, is a celebration of originality, innovation, and the spirit of humanitarianism. It showcases how Aquarian traits can challenge the status quo, introduce revolutionary ideas, and ultimately lead to the betterment of society. The Eleventh Doctor, as The Innovator, embodies the essence of Aquarius, proving that with creativity, vision, and a commitment to the greater good, even the most entrenched societal norms can be transformed for the better.

Chapter 12: Pisces - The Twelfth Doctor (The Mystic)

In the boundless tapestry of the cosmos, there exists a realm that defies the conventional laws of space and time. Known as the Dreamscape, this realm is a nexus of raw emotions, hopes, and fears, a place where the physical and the ethereal merge into an ever-shifting landscape of surreal beauty and hidden dangers. It is within this dream-like realm that the Twelfth Doctor, embodying the profound empathy, intuition, and mystical qualities of Pisces, embarks on a quest to rescue lost souls ensnared by their deepest fears and unfulfilled desires.

The Twelfth Doctor, with his piercing gaze and enigmatic presence, personifies the essence of Pisces. He is the Mystic, a being of deep understanding and compassion, qualities that are essential for navigating the Dreamscape. His journey is not one of physical travel but of spiritual and emotional exploration, a voyage into the heart of what it means to dream and to despair.

The challenge the Doctor faces in the Dreamscape is unlike any other. The lost souls he seeks to rescue are trapped within their own personal nightmares, unable to awaken or escape. These souls, a diverse array of individuals from countless worlds and times, are bound by a common thread of unresolved emotional turmoil. The entity that rules over the Dreamscape, known as the Weaver, feeds on this turmoil, weaving it into the fabric of the realm to strengthen its control.

To confront the Weaver and liberate the lost souls, the Doctor must delve deep into the essence of Pisces. He employs his extraordinary empathy to connect with each soul, entering their nightmares to understand and confront the fears that hold them captive. His approach is one of compassion and understanding, using his intuitive grasp of the human condition to guide these souls toward a realization of their own strength and potential for overcoming their despair.

The Doctor's journey through the Dreamscape is a series of poignant encounters that test the limits of his empathy and mystic insight. In one instance, he navigates the labyrinthine mind of a soldier haunted by the horrors of war, helping him find peace with his past. In another, he ventures into the dreams of a young alien child, lost and alone, her nightmares a reflection of her fear of abandonment. Through each encounter, the Doctor's Piscean qualities shine through, his deep connection with the emotional and spiritual dimensions guiding him and those he seeks to save.

As the Doctor draws closer to confronting the Weaver, the Dreamscape reveals its ultimate truth: that it is a reflection of the collective unconscious, a realm shaped by the dreams and fears of all sentient beings. The Weaver's power is derived from the suppression of hope, the stifling of the spirit that dreams of a better tomorrow.

The confrontation with the Weaver becomes a battle not of strength but of spirit. The Doctor, wielding the mystical and empathetic powers of Pisces, challenges the Weaver's narrative of despair with a vision of hope and unity. He unites the dreams of the lost souls into a collective force of positive emotion, their combined willpower and dreams overpowering the Weaver's hold on the Dreamscape.

In the aftermath of the Weaver's defeat, the Dreamscape is transformed. No longer a prison of fear, it becomes a sanctuary of healing and understanding, a place where lost souls can find solace and guidance. The Doctor, having navigated the deepest recesses of the human psyche, leaves the Dreamscape with a renewed sense of purpose, his belief in the power of dreams and the resilience of the spirit reaffirmed.

Chapter 12 of "Doctor Who Astrology," featuring the Twelfth Doctor as Pisces, is a testament to the power of empathy, intuition, and the mystical connection that binds all living beings. It showcases the Piscean qualities of spiritual depth, compassion, and the understanding that in the dreams and fears of each individual lies the universal truth of our shared humanity. The Twelfth Doctor, as The Mystic, embodies the essence of Pisces, guiding lost souls through the shadows of despair and into the light of hope and redemption.

Conclusion: The Cosmic Alignment

As the threads of destiny weave together the tapestry of time and space, a moment of unprecedented cosmic alignment approaches. This alignment, foretold by ancient civilizations and whispered among the stars, holds the power to unravel the fabric of the universe itself. It is a convergence that calls for balance, for the harmonization of energies that span the breadth of existence. In response to this celestial summons, all incarnations of the Doctor, each a reflection of the zodiac's multifaceted essence, come together in a union of purpose and will. This gathering is not just a meeting of individuals but a confluence of traits, experiences, and philosophies, each Doctor bringing forth the strengths and insights of their guiding signs.

The cosmic alignment serves as a crucible, within which the interconnectedness and balance of the zodiac signs are laid bare. The Aries' pioneering courage, the Taurus' steadfast resolve, Gemini's adaptable intellect, Cancer's nurturing empathy, Leo's heroic heart, Virgo's meticulous analysis, Libra's diplomatic grace, Scorpio's transformative depth, Sagittarius' boundless exploration, Capricorn's disciplined ambition, Aquarius' revolutionary vision, and Pisces' mystical intuition—all these qualities blend into a singular force capable of confronting the cosmic upheaval.

As the Doctors navigate the complexities of the alignment, their journey is a reflection on the importance of understanding and embracing the diverse aspects of one's character. It becomes evident that the challenges posed by the alignment cannot be overcome by any single trait or approach. Instead, it is the synergy of qualities, the ability to adapt and draw upon the strength needed for the moment, that holds the key to preserving the balance of the universe.

This unity of purpose among the Doctors, despite their diverse personalities and approaches, underscores a fundamental truth: that within each individual lies a universe of potential, a constellation of traits that, when embraced and balanced, can navigate the most daunting challenges. The cosmic alignment, with its threat to the fabric of reality, becomes a catalyst for a deeper understanding of the self and the power of unity in diversity.

The resolution of the cosmic alignment is not just a victory over a cosmic threat but a testament to the strength found in balance and harmony. As the Doctors part ways, returning to their own times and spaces, they carry with them a renewed sense of purpose and an understanding that the diversity of the universe, like the diversity within each individual, is not a source of division but a wellspring of strength.

The conclusion of "Doctor Who Astrology" is a celebration of the journey through the zodiac, an odyssey that illuminates the interconnectedness of all things. It is a reminder that the cosmos, in its infinite diversity and complexity, mirrors the depths of the human spirit. Through the lens of astrology and the adventures of the Doctor, we are invited to explore the myriad aspects of our own characters, to embrace the totality of our being, and to recognize that in the grand scheme of the universe, balance and harmony are not just ideals but the very foundations of existence.

In this cosmic dance of alignments and energies, the Doctors stand as guardians of balance, their stories a testament to the enduring power of unity in diversity. "Doctor Who Astrology" thus concludes not just as a narrative of cosmic adventure but as an invitation to each of us to explore the universe within, to embrace our complexities, and to navigate the starlit path of our destinies with courage, wisdom, and an open heart.

Epilogue: The Universe's Symphony

In the quiet aftermath of the cosmic alignment, the universe breathes a sigh of relief. Stars twinkle a little brighter, the fabric of reality settles into a harmonious rhythm, and the cosmos itself seems to hum with a newfound vibrancy. This is the symphony of the universe, a melody composed of the countless adventures, trials, and triumphs of those who stand as its guardians. Among these guardians, the Doctors, each an echo of the zodiac's vast spectrum, continue their eternal journey through time and space, their destinies forever intertwined in the cosmos's vast and mysterious tapestry.

The universe, now in harmony, reveals the subtle but profound changes wrought by the cosmic alignment and the actions of the Doctors. Worlds on the brink of conflict find paths to peace; civilizations facing environmental collapse discover solutions; and across the galaxies, the seeds of understanding and cooperation take root. These are not utopias, for challenges remain, but they are worlds where hope shines a bit brighter, where the potential for growth and learning is ever-present.

The Doctors, too, are transformed by the experience. Each, in embodying the strengths of their zodiac signs, has not only contributed to the balance of the universe but has also delved deeper into their own essence. The Aries Doctor, emboldened by courage; the Taurus, more steadfast than ever; Gemini, embracing the power of communication and adaptability; Cancer, finding strength in empathy; Leo, shining with heroic brilliance; Virgo, grounded in meticulous care; Libra, a beacon of harmony; Scorpio, a wellspring of transformative depth; Sagittarius, ignited with the flame of exploration; Capricorn, resolute in their ambition; Aquarius, visionary and revolutionary; and Pisces, a mystic with a heart open to the infinite—all stand as luminaries in the universe's ever-expanding story.

As they continue their adventures, the ripple effects of their unity and individual strengths are felt across the cosmos. Planets whisper tales of the Doctors, legends that speak to the heart of every being that hears them. These stories, rich with the wisdom and courage of the Doctors, inspire others to look beyond their horizons, to question, to dream, and to explore. The universe becomes a place of infinite possibilities, where every star, every planet, every creature plays a part in the symphony of existence.

The universe's symphony is not a static melody but an ever-evolving composition. It speaks of the past, with its challenges and triumphs, and of the future, with its endless potential for growth and discovery. The Doctors, with their zodiac-inspired strengths, continue to weave through this melody, separate but forever connected by the cosmic web that binds all things.

In the epilogue of "Doctor Who Astrology," the universe stands as a testament to the power of harmony and balance. It is a reflection on the beauty of diversity and the strength found in unity. As the cosmos moves forward, its symphony echoing through the void, it carries with it the legacy of the Doctors—a legacy of courage, compassion, and an unyielding desire to explore and protect. Their adventures, a microcosm of the universe's vast tapestry, remind us that we, too, are part of this symphony, each of us a unique note in the grand chorus of existence.

And so, the universe spins on, its mysteries and wonders endless, its symphony a celebration of life in all its forms. The Doctors, guardians of this cosmic dance, continue their journey, their stories interwoven with the fabric of time and space, eternal and inspiring. "Doctor Who Astrology" closes on a note of hope and anticipation, a reminder that in the grand, intricate design of the universe, every moment is an opportunity for adventure, for learning, and for growth.

Section 2

\-

\-

\-

\-

\-

\-

Message from The Author

Hello,

For this next section we are going to take a look at celestial events such as Solar Flares, Eclipses, etc. In fact, as the time of writing this, there is an Eclipse is happening in the United States around Texas, on April 8th, 2024.

Let us begin our Journey on to Section 2.

Introduction

Doctor Who, the timeless British science fiction series, has captivated audiences around the globe with its unique blend of adventure, mystery, and the exploration of the human condition through the lens of the extraterrestrial. At the heart of this beloved series is the Doctor, an enigmatic Time Lord from the planet Gallifrey, with the extraordinary ability to travel through time and space in the TARDIS, a ship camouflaged as a British police box from the 1960s. This ability sets the stage for boundless storytelling possibilities, allowing the Doctor to intersect with countless civilizations, historical moments, and cosmic phenomena. The central charm of Doctor Who lies not just in the thrilling escapades or the advanced technology but in the Doctor's profound connection with beings across the universe, often standing as a guardian against the forces of darkness and tyranny.

Astrology, a system of beliefs and traditions that humans have looked to for guidance and understanding for millennia, offers a fascinating lens through which to view our place in the cosmos. Rooted in the movements and relative positions of celestial bodies, astrology posits that these cosmic dances have a direct influence on human affairs and terrestrial events. Throughout history, from ancient Babylon to the Renaissance and beyond, astrology has been a significant cultural force, shaping art, politics, and society. Its symbols and archetypes continue to resonate with millions today, reflecting a deep, enduring human urge to find harmony and meaning in the vast, mysterious universe.

In a groundbreaking Doctor Who storyline, the time-honored realms of science fiction and astrology converge, introducing a captivating narrative arc that explores the significance of astrology in the broader cosmos. A mysterious astrological alignment, unseen for millennia, emerges as a harbinger of chaos, threatening the very fabric of the universe. This celestial event, powerful and enigmatic, draws the Doctor into a cosmic detective story that spans the breadth of time and space. As the alignment nears, its potential to warp reality and unravel the threads of existence becomes increasingly apparent, compelling the Doctor to delve deep into ancient astrological lore, alien civilizations that have harnessed the stars in unthinkable ways, and the hidden connections between the universe's most mysterious forces.

Embarking on this quest, the Doctor confronts not only the physical manifestations of this astrological phenomenon but also its profound philosophical implications. What is the role of destiny in the cosmos? Can the movements of celestial bodies truly presage cataclysmic events, or is the universe more chaotic and unpredictable than we, or even the Doctor, can imagine? This storyline promises to be a mesmerizing fusion of science fiction and mystical astrology, challenging the Doctor to navigate the intricate web of cosmic fate and free will, in a quest to safeguard the universe from an unprecedented astral catastrophe. Through this journey, Doctor Who continues to enchant with its boundless imagination, while inviting viewers to ponder the ancient and ever-pertinent question of our place among the stars.

Chapter 1: The Cosmic Call

In the vast silence of the cosmos, a series of cryptic signals pierced the void, cutting through the endless chatter of the universe like a beacon in the night. These were not the usual communications intercepted by the TARDIS, the Doctor's time-traveling ship. They were complex, patterned, and unmistakably deliberate, resembling ancient astrological symbols more than any known language or code. The Doctor, ever curious and unbound by the constraints of time and space, was immediately captivated. These symbols, radiating from an uncharted sector of the universe, hinted at knowledge and mysteries that even the Doctor could not ignore.

As the TARDIS hummed with the energy of these mysterious signals, the Doctor was joined by a new companion, Alex, an amateur astrologer with a keen intellect and a boundless fascination for the stars. Alex, with their deep understanding of celestial symbols and their historical significance, recognized the patterns as a distress call, encoded in the ancient language of astrology. The symbols were not random; they told a story of alignment, disruption, and a plea for help that transcended the boundaries of time and space.

The Doctor, impressed by Alex's insight, felt a spark of excitement at the prospect of an adventure that bridged the gap between the empirical and the mystical. The TARDIS, ever responsive to the Doctor's will, began to chart a course toward the source of the signals. The decision was made: they would answer the cosmic call, embarking on a journey that promised to unravel the mysteries of the universe through the lens of astrology.

As the TARDIS dematerialized, leaving behind the familiar swirl of time and space, the Doctor and Alex prepared themselves for what lay ahead. This was no ordinary mission; it was a voyage into the unknown, where the ancient wisdom of the stars would guide them toward a destiny that was written in the heavens long before the Doctor had ever set foot on Earth.

The journey to the source of the signals was fraught with anticipation. Alex, with their star charts and astrological texts, worked alongside the Doctor, decoding the messages that continued to guide their path. Each symbol, from the fierce ram of Aries to the scales of Libra, seemed to hold a key to understanding the nature of the distress call. It was as if the universe itself was speaking in the language of the stars, beckoning the Doctor and Alex to intervene in an event of cosmic significance.

As they neared their destination, the Doctor and Alex could feel the fabric of space becoming strained, as if the very threads of reality were being twisted by the gravitational pull of the impending astrological alignment. The TARDIS, sensitive to the shifts in the cosmic balance, shuddered as they approached the source of the signals.

Stepping out of the TARDIS, the Doctor and Alex found themselves on a planet that defied all expectations. It was a world where the skies were alive with the glow of countless stars, each one pulsating with the energy of the celestial bodies they represented. The air was charged with a palpable tension, as if the planet itself was aware of the monumental astrological event that was about to unfold.

In the distance, a figure stood, silhouetted against the starlit horizon. This was the sender of the signals, the keeper of the astrological secrets that had called the Doctor and Alex across the universe. As they approached, the figure turned, revealing themselves to be an astrologer of unparalleled knowledge, whose understanding of the cosmos had foreseen the coming disruption.

With the meeting of minds between the Doctor, Alex, and the astrologer, the stage was set for an adventure that would challenge their understanding of the universe. Together, they would delve into the mysteries of the astrological alignment, deciphering its significance and confronting the forces that sought to use it for their own ends.

Thus began the cosmic call, an invitation to journey beyond the known, guided by the stars and bound by the shared destiny of those who answer when the universe reaches out in its time of need.

Chapter 2: The Zodiac Constellations

The TARDIS, with its uncanny ability to breach the veil between the seen and the unseen, materialized on a planet where the constellations were not merely patterns in the sky but living, breathing entities. This world was a cosmic tapestry, where each constellation was a domain, imbued with the essence and challenges reflective of its astrological significance. Here, the stars did not just twinkle from afar; they invited you into their stories, demanding to be lived, understood, and overcome.

As the Doctor and Alex stepped out into the crisp air of this celestial realm, they were immediately enveloped in a landscape that shimmered with astral energy. The ground beneath their feet was alive with patterns of starlight, mirroring the constellations that danced overhead in the night sky. It was a place of profound beauty and equally profound mystery, where each step forward was a step into the heart of the zodiac.

Aries: The Challenge of Initiation and Courage

Their first encounter was with Aries, the ram, a constellation that pulsed with the fiery energy of initiation and courage. The Doctor, with a twinkle of excitement in their eyes, and Alex, with an eager anticipation, found themselves at the beginning of a winding path. This path, marked by the glowing symbols of Aries, promised a trial of bravery and leadership, traits embodied by the ram.

As they navigated the path, the landscape around them transformed. They were no longer merely travelers but leaders of a charge against unseen forces, embodying the pioneering spirit of Aries. The challenge here was not to conquer with brute force but to lead with courage, to inspire others to follow where fear might otherwise prevail. It was a test of will, where the first steps of their journey mirrored the initiation rites of heroes of old.

Taurus: The Puzzle of Persistence and Revelation

Having proven their mettle in the domain of Aries, the Doctor and Alex advanced to the realm of Taurus, the bull. Here, the vibrant, earthy energy of Taurus enveloped them, grounding their spirits after the fiery trial of Aries. Taurus, with its association with persistence, patience, and revelation, offered a different kind of challenge—a puzzle that required not just physical endurance but the strength of will to uncover deeper truths.

The landscape of Taurus was a labyrinthine garden, teeming with life and the rich, fertile essence of the earth. The paths, bordered by towering hedges, twisted and turned in seemingly endless configurations, each dead end a lesson in patience and perseverance. The Doctor, with their infinite curiosity, and Alex, with their keen astrological insight, worked in tandem, unraveling the secrets of the maze. The key, they discovered, was not merely to navigate the labyrinth but to understand it, to see beyond the immediate path and grasp the deeper significance of their journey.

At the heart of the maze, they encountered the Guardian of Taurus, a being of majestic stature, whose eyes held the depth of centuries. The Guardian presented them with a riddle, an ancient verse that spoke of the earth's bounty and the enduring strength of the spirit. Solving the riddle required not just intellect but an appreciation for the slow, relentless power of nature—the same power that shapes mountains and carves rivers.

With the riddle solved, the Guardian bestowed upon them a gift: a revelation that would illuminate their path forward. It was a glimpse of the interconnectedness of all things, a reminder that strength is not always found in action but often in the quiet, persistent growth of understanding and wisdom.

As the Doctor and Alex emerged from the realm of Taurus, they carried with them the lessons of the zodiac's first two constellations: the courage to begin and the persistence to delve deeper. Ahead of them lay the remaining constellations, each promising its own challenges and revelations, a cosmic journey through the essence of human experience, guided by the stars themselves.

Gemini: The Labyrinth of Communication and Duality

Having traversed the realms of Aries and Taurus, the Doctor and Alex found themselves stepping into the vibrant essence of Gemini, the twins. This domain was immediately different from the previous ones; it was a place of air, movement, and light, embodying the mutable qualities of communication, intellect, and duality that Gemini represents.

The terrain before them morphed into a bustling cityscape, alive with the buzz of countless conversations, the exchange of ideas, and the swift movement of information. The challenge in Gemini was not to navigate physical obstacles but to navigate the complexities of communication and understanding in a place where every voice carried a different story, a different perspective.

The Doctor, with their adeptness at unraveling the intricate tapestries of alien societies, and Alex, with their human intuition and adaptability, found themselves at the heart of a puzzle that required them to understand and reconcile opposing viewpoints. The city was divided, its inhabitants locked in a perpetual debate, a reflection of Gemini's dual nature.

The task at hand was to bridge this divide, to find a common ground in a place where contradiction was the norm. It was a test of diplomacy and insight, requiring the Doctor and Alex to employ their skills in empathy and negotiation. They moved through the city, engaging with its denizens, listening to their stories, and gradually weaving a narrative that highlighted their shared concerns and dreams.

The culmination of their efforts was a grand council, where all sides came together to listen and be heard. The Doctor and Alex facilitated this exchange, demonstrating the power of communication to heal and unite. It was a delicate dance of words and ideas, a balancing act that mirrored the duality of Gemini itself.

In the end, the resolution they brokered did not erase the differences between the city's factions but instead celebrated them, fostering a new understanding that diversity of thought and perspective was not a barrier but a strength. The Gemini constellation, with its emphasis on the connection between individuals and ideas, taught them that true communication requires not just the transmission of information but the willingness to listen and embrace the multifaceted nature of existence.

As they left Gemini behind, the Doctor and Alex reflected on the lessons learned. They had navigated the labyrinth of communication, faced the challenge of duality, and emerged with a deeper appreciation for the complex interplay of voices and perspectives that shape our understanding of the world. Ahead lay the next constellation, each step forward a step deeper into the cosmic exploration of the human spirit, guided by the stars' ancient wisdom.

Cancer: The Sanctuary of Emotion and Protection

After the bustling intellectualism of Gemini, the TARDIS led the Doctor and Alex into the constellation of Cancer, the crab. This realm immediately enveloped them in a serene, luminous glow, suggestive of the moon's gentle light, Cancer's ruling celestial body. Here, the energy shifted towards the introspective and nurturing, focusing on the themes of emotion, protection, and the concept of home.

The landscape transformed into a vast, tranquil sea, reflecting the moon's soft light. Small islands dotted the horizon, each one a sanctuary representing the intimate, protective embrace of Cancer. The challenge in Cancer's domain was not one of intellect or physical prowess but of understanding the depth of emotion and the strength found in vulnerability and care.

As they navigated these waters, the Doctor and Alex encountered individuals and creatures whose stories were etched with the need for protection, love, and understanding. Each island brought them closer to comprehending the complex web of relationships that define a home and a community, emphasizing the importance of emotional bonds and the care we owe to one another.

The central challenge emerged on an island at the heart of the sea, where a community was fractured by fear and misunderstanding, their protective instincts turned inward, isolating them from each other.

The Doctor and Alex, drawing upon the lessons of Cancer, worked to heal these divides, showing that true strength lies in mutual care and protection, not in isolation.

This task involved not just diplomatic skill but emotional intelligence, requiring them to listen deeply and respond with empathy. They facilitated dialogues, mediated conflicts, and gently guided the community towards a renewed sense of unity and purpose. It was a delicate operation, akin to nurturing a garden, where each individual needed specific care to flourish.

In the process, the Doctor and Alex were also reminded of their own vulnerabilities and the importance of having a safe space to return to, a theme that resonated deeply with the Doctor, who had seen countless worlds but always found solace in the TARDIS, their own cosmic sanctuary.

By the time they were ready to depart, the community had begun to rebuild, not just their homes but their relationships with each other, grounded in mutual respect and understanding. The Doctor and Alex left behind a place transformed, a testament to the healing power of empathy and the protective strength of love.

Cancer's realm taught them the value of emotional depth, the courage it takes to show care, and the fundamental human need for connection and protection. These lessons, carried in their hearts, prepared them for the challenges ahead as they continued their journey through the zodiac constellations, each step an exploration of the multifaceted human experience, guided by the celestial wisdom of the stars.

Leo: The Arena of Expression and Valor

Leaving the nurturing shores of Cancer behind, the Doctor and Alex were next drawn into the vibrant constellation of Leo, where the essence of the sun—Leo's ruling body—permeated every aspect of this new realm. Here, they were met with a landscape that dazzled the senses, a kingdom where the golden light of creativity, pride, and bravery shone brightly. Leo's domain was an endless summer's day, filled with the roars of applause and the thrill of performance, a testament to the constellation's association with expression, recognition, and the courage to stand out.

The challenge within Leo's realm was unique, focusing on the art of genuine expression and the valor required to face one's fears in the spotlight. The Doctor and Alex found themselves at the center of a grand amphitheater, surrounded by an audience of diverse beings from across the universe, all eager to witness the spectacle of courage and creativity that defined Leo's spirit.

The task set before them was to engage in the Great Performance, a tradition in this part of the cosmos where individuals showcased their talents, not for accolades, but as a celebration of their innate creativity and strength. It was a challenge that required them to tap into their most authentic selves, to perform with heart and valor in a way that resonated with the essence of Leo.

The Doctor, with centuries of experiences spanning countless cultures and epochs, chose to weave a tale through an intricate dance of time and space, using the TARDIS's technology to project images of the universe's wonders, captivating the audience with the beauty and diversity of existence. It was a performance that highlighted the Doctor's own journey, a celebration of life's complexity and the bravery required to embrace it fully.

Alex, drawing upon their deep love for astrology and the stories written in the stars, shared a narrative that connected the celestial patterns to the personal, weaving a tapestry that illustrated how the stars' movements mirrored the human quest for meaning and belonging. Their performance, though quieter, was no less impactful, touching the hearts of all who watched, reminding them of the interconnectedness of all things.

Their performances, so different yet equally sincere, were met with thunderous applause, not for the spectacle, but for the genuine expression of self that each had dared to reveal. In Leo's realm, they learned the importance of standing in one's truth, the strength found in vulnerability, and the joy of sharing one's inner light with the world.

As they left the amphitheater, the Doctor and Alex carried with them the warmth of Leo's sun, a reminder that true bravery lies in the courage to be oneself, and that recognition and respect are earned not by seeking the spotlight, but by the authenticity and passion one brings to their life's performance.

The journey through the zodiac constellations continued, with each step uncovering deeper layers of the human spirit, guided by the celestial wisdom that connected them all. Leo's lessons in courage, creativity, and the importance of self-expression would illuminate their path as they ventured further into the mysteries of the stars.

Virgo: The Garden of Service and Detail

After the grandeur and warmth of Leo, the TARDIS next navigated the intricate and thoughtful constellation of Virgo. Here, the environment transformed dramatically, revealing a vast, meticulously tended garden that stretched to the horizon, under a soft, clear sky. This realm was a reflection of Virgo's essence: precision, service, and an unwavering attention to detail. The garden was not just a place of beauty, but a living symbol of the Virgoan dedication to nurturing, improvement, and the harmonious balance of nature.

Upon arrival, the Doctor and Alex were greeted by the Keepers of the Garden, beings who embodied Virgo's ideals. They explained that the challenge in Virgo's domain was to aid in the restoration and balance of the garden, which had fallen into disarray due to a recent cosmic event. The task required not just hard work, but a discerning eye and a gentle hand, qualities that resonated deeply with Virgo's spirit of service and perfectionism.

The Doctor, with a natural inclination towards solving puzzles, immediately engaged with the problem, analyzing the garden's layout and the natural laws that governed its existence. Alex, on the other hand, used their knowledge of astrology to understand the cosmic influences at play, offering insights into how the garden's harmony could be restored in alignment with the stars.

Together, they set to work, tending to the garden with care and precision. They pruned overgrown areas, repaired damaged structures, and introduced new plant species that would bring balance to the ecosystem. It was a laborious task, requiring patience and a keen attention to detail, but as the garden began to flourish once again, the Doctor and Alex found satisfaction in the tangible results of their efforts.

In the process, they learned the importance of Virgo's virtues: the value of meticulous care, the joy of service, and the beauty that emerges from attention to detail. The garden became a testament to the idea that even the smallest actions, performed with intention and care, can have a profound impact on the world around us.

The Keepers of the Garden, impressed by the Doctor and Alex's dedication, rewarded them with a gift: a rare flower that bloomed only under the light of a specific constellation, symbolizing the interconnectedness of all things and the importance of every detail in the tapestry of the cosmos.

As they departed Virgo's domain, the Doctor and Alex carried with them the lessons of the garden: that true service is a form of love, that perfection is not an end but a journey, and that in the meticulous care of the small, one can find the keys to the balance and health of the whole.

Their journey through the zodiac constellations continued, each constellation offering new insights and challenges, weaving together a journey that explored the depth and complexity of the human experience, guided by the ancient wisdom of the stars. Virgo's lesson in service and detail would serve as a grounding force as they ventured into the mysteries yet to be revealed by the remaining constellations.

Libra: The Scales of Harmony and Decision

Leaving behind the meticulous gardens of Virgo, the Doctor and Alex next found themselves under the influence of Libra, the scales. This constellation's domain manifested as a breathtaking city of balance and symmetry, reflecting Libra's association with harmony, justice, and the art of decision-making. The architecture was a marvel of equilibrium, with every structure designed to reflect the duality and fairness that are core to Libra's essence.

Upon their arrival, they were welcomed by the Arbiters of Libra, beings who maintained the delicate balance of the city through wise governance and judicious decision-making. The Doctor and Alex were informed that their challenge in this realm would be to resolve a long-standing dispute that threatened the harmony of the city. This conflict, deeply rooted in the history of the Libran domain, required a resolution that would not only address the immediate discord but also restore the balance so crucial to the city's survival.

The Doctor, with their vast experience in mediating cosmic disputes, and Alex, with their inherent understanding of human (and non-human) nature, dove into the heart of the conflict. They listened to the grievances of all parties involved, seeking to understand the complexities and nuances of the situation. The challenge lay not in identifying a winner or a loser but in finding a solution that all could accept, a path forward that would mend the rift and bring about a greater understanding among the city's inhabitants.

The process was intricate, involving negotiation, empathy, and a deep appreciation for the art of compromise. The Doctor and Alex employed their skills to highlight common ground and foster a sense of shared purpose. They worked tirelessly, facilitating discussions that led to revelations and, eventually, reconciliation. The solution they proposed was innovative, a testament to the creative potential that arises from seeking balance and understanding.

In resolving the dispute, the Doctor and Alex not only restored peace to the Libran city but also deepened their own understanding of the importance of balance in all aspects of life. Libra's domain taught them that true harmony arises not from suppressing conflict but from addressing it with fairness and an open heart. They learned that every decision shapes the future, and that finding equilibrium in a world of chaos is an art form in itself.

As they bid farewell to the Arbiters of Libra, the Doctor and Alex were gifted a symbol of the city's gratitude: a medallion bearing the scales of Libra, a reminder of the equilibrium they had helped to restore and the delicate balance that governs all relationships.

With the lessons of Libra etched into their spirits, the Doctor and Alex continued their journey through the zodiac constellations, each encounter enriching their voyage with deeper insights into the complexities of the universe and the myriad ways in which balance, in its many forms, underpins the cosmic dance.

Scorpio: The Depths of Transformation and Mystery

After the harmonious and balanced vistas of Libra, the TARDIS spiraled into the intense and shadowy realm of Scorpio. This domain was starkly different, embodying the enigmatic, transformative essence of Scorpio. Here, the Doctor and Alex found themselves in a landscape that pulsed with a powerful, magnetic energy, an environment that beckoned them to look beyond the surface and dive into the mysteries that lay hidden in the shadows.

The setting was a vast, twilight realm, where perpetual dusk cast long shadows over land and water alike. It was a place of secrets, of deep waters and deeper caves, where the truths of the universe whispered from the dark corners of existence. The challenge in Scorpio's domain was not just to confront these mysteries but to undergo a process of transformation, to face one's own inner depths and emerge changed.

The inhabitants of this realm were the Custodians of the Deep, enigmatic beings who guarded the secrets of Scorpio with a solemn duty. They presented the Doctor and Alex with a quest: to retrieve a lost artifact, the Scorpion's Sting, an ancient relic said to hold the power of ultimate truth but hidden in the heart of the most treacherous depths.

The journey to retrieve the artifact was a trial by fire and water, leading the Doctor and Alex through landscapes that tested their resolve and courage. They navigated dark waters, where unseen creatures lurked, and traversed caverns where the slightest misstep could be their undoing. Each step forward required not just physical bravery but the willingness to confront the psychological shadows that Scorpio brought to the surface.

As they delved deeper, the Doctor and Alex encountered trials that forced them to confront their fears and doubts, challenges that mirrored Scorpio's themes of death and rebirth. These trials were not cruel but served to strip away illusions, revealing the core of their beings and the strength that lies in vulnerability and acceptance of change.

When they finally discovered the Scorpion's Sting, it was not in the form they had expected. Instead of a tangible artifact, they found a pool of water, still and deep, that reflected their true selves back at them. The real treasure was the transformation they had undergone, the understanding that the deepest truths lie within oneself, and that facing one's shadows is the path to discovering one's light.

With this revelation, the Doctor and Alex were able to return to the Custodians of the Deep, not with an object, but with a profound personal transformation. The Custodians, recognizing the depth of their journey, declared the trial complete, affirming that the true power of Scorpio lies in the metamorphosis of the soul.

As they left Scorpio's realm, the Doctor and Alex carried with them the lessons of the depths: that transformation is the essence of life, that truth requires the courage to confront the darkness, and that rebirth is born from the acceptance of one's entire self, shadows and all.

Their journey through the zodiac constellations continued, each constellation revealing new dimensions of existence, guided by the ancient wisdom of the stars. Scorpio's lesson in transformation and the embracing of the mysterious depths of life would illuminate their path as they ventured into the challenges that awaited in the constellations to come.

Sagittarius: The Odyssey of Exploration and Wisdom

Following the transformative depths of Scorpio, the Doctor and Alex embarked on the next phase of their celestial journey, entering the realm of Sagittarius. This domain was imbued with the spirit of the adventurer, a vast, unbounded landscape that beckoned to the heart of the explorer, promising the thrill of discovery and the pursuit of wisdom. Here, the essence of Sagittarius—a mutable fire sign known for its love of freedom, exploration, and the search for meaning—was palpable in the air, stirring the souls of the Doctor and Alex with a sense of boundless possibility.

The environment before them was a dynamic tapestry of diverse terrains, from lush, sprawling jungles to vast deserts and towering mountains, each region offering its own mysteries and adventures. The challenge in Sagittarius' realm was not a singular quest but an odyssey—a series of journeys, each with its own lessons and trials, reflecting Sagittarius's association with the philosopher and the seeker.

Their guide in this expansive world was the Archer, a figure who embodied the Sagittarian spirit of aspiration and pursuit. The Archer invited the Doctor and Alex to partake in the Great Hunt, a metaphorical journey that would lead them across the various landscapes of Sagittarius, challenging them to grow in wisdom and understanding with each leg of their journey.

The first leg of the Great Hunt led them through the jungles of Insight, where ancient ruins whispered secrets of long-forgotten civilizations. Here, the Doctor's keen intellect and Alex's astrological knowledge were put to the test as they deciphered clues hidden in the stars and the stones, uncovering wisdom that spoke to the interconnectedness of all life and the importance of understanding our place in the universe.

Next, they traversed the Deserts of Reflection, a place where the vast, open skies and the endless sands forced them to confront their own inner landscapes. The solitude and the silence of the desert offered a space for introspection, challenging them to look within and question their beliefs, desires, and the very essence of their journey.

The final challenge took them to the Mountains of Aspiration, towering peaks that represented the pinnacle of Sagittarian pursuit—the quest for the ultimate truth. Climbing these mountains required not just physical strength but the courage to face the unknown and the willingness to keep seeking, even when the path was fraught with obstacles.

With each leg of the Great Hunt, the Doctor and Alex grew in wisdom and understanding, learning that the true essence of Sagittarius lies not in the destination but in the journey itself. The Archer, impressed by their perseverance and insight, rewarded them with the Arrow of Sagittarius, a symbol of their journey and a reminder that the quest for knowledge and truth is an ever-evolving path.

As they bid farewell to the realm of Sagittarius, the Doctor and Alex carried with them the spirit of the adventurer and the wisdom of the philosopher. Their odyssey through Sagittarius had taught them the value of exploration, not just of the world around them but of the vast, uncharted territories within their own souls.

Their journey through the zodiac constellations continued, each constellation offering new insights into the cosmos and the human condition, guided by the ancient wisdom of the stars. Sagittarius's lesson in exploration and the pursuit of wisdom would light their way as they ventured forth into the mysteries that awaited them in the final constellations.

Capricorn: The Ascent of Ambition and Mastery

After the expansive odyssey through Sagittarius, the Doctor and Alex approached the realm of Capricorn. This domain manifested as a rugged, mountainous terrain that towered into the clouds, a stark embodiment of Capricorn's association with ambition, discipline, and the pursuit of mastery. The atmosphere here was charged with a sobering, earthy energy, grounding them after the boundless adventures of Sagittarius. In Capricorn, the journey was upward, a metaphorical climb towards the peaks of personal and professional achievement.

The guiding force in this realm was the Seer of the Summit, a wise and venerable figure who had mastered the arts of patience, persistence, and resilience—qualities that Capricorn held in high esteem. The Seer welcomed the Doctor and Alex, presenting them with the challenge of Capricorn: to ascend the Mountain of Endeavor, a peak that symbolized the pinnacle of one's aspirations and the culmination of hard work and dedication.

The ascent was daunting, a physical and metaphorical representation of the struggles one faces on the path to achieving greatness. The mountain was steep, the paths narrow and fraught with obstacles. Each phase of the climb tested their resolve, demanding not just physical strength but a steadfast commitment to their goals.

The Doctor, with a spirit tempered by countless lifetimes of challenges, led the way with unwavering determination. Alex, drawing upon the inner strength they had discovered through their journey among the stars, followed closely, their resolve fortified by the trials they had overcome. Together, they faced the mountain, embodying the Capricornian virtues of discipline and perseverance.

As they climbed, the Seer of the Summit appeared to them at intervals, offering wisdom and insight to aid their journey. They learned the importance of setting concrete goals, of planning and preparation, and of the resilience required to overcome setbacks. The Seer taught them that true mastery is not achieved in the absence of struggle, but through the continuous effort to rise above one's limitations.

The summit, when they finally reached it, offered a breathtaking view that stretched across the cosmos, a fitting reward for their toil. But the true prize was not the view, nor was it the end of their ascent; it was the realization of their own growth and the mastery they had achieved over themselves.

The Seer of the Summit, acknowledging their success, bestowed upon them the Capstone of Capricorn, a symbol of their achievement and the culmination of their efforts. It was a reminder that the greatest accomplishments are those earned through dedication, hard work, and the unwavering pursuit of one's goals.

With the lessons of Capricorn etched into their beings, the Doctor and Alex descended the mountain, their spirits enriched by the experience. They carried with them the understanding that ambition, when guided by discipline and tempered by wisdom, can lead to the highest forms of personal fulfillment and achievement.

Their celestial journey was nearing its conclusion, with only a few constellations left to explore. The wisdom of Capricorn, with its focus on ambition and the ascent to mastery, would serve as a foundation for the challenges and discoveries that lay ahead, guiding them as they continued to navigate the cosmos, driven by the ancient wisdom of the stars.

Aquarius: The Waters of Innovation and Unity

Emerging from the disciplined climbs of Capricorn, the Doctor and Alex next found themselves entering the realm of Aquarius. This domain unfolded as a futuristic metropolis, brimming with innovation and a sense of community that transcended traditional boundaries. Aquarius, with its association with forward-thinking, revolution, and the collective well-being, painted a stark contrast to the solitary ascent of Capricorn. Here, the focus shifted from personal ambition to the ideals of progress and unity that could benefit all of society.

The cityscape of Aquarius was a marvel of technological advancement and architectural ingenuity, reflecting the sign's affinity for breakthroughs and the unconventional. The air buzzed with the energy of collective endeavors and the sharing of ideas, a testament to Aquarius's ruling element, air, which symbolizes communication and intellect.

Upon their arrival, the Doctor and Alex were greeted by the Visionaries of Aquarius, a group dedicated to harnessing innovation for the betterment of the universe. The challenge presented in this realm was to contribute to a grand project, one that aimed to solve a critical issue affecting not just the city but countless civilizations across the stars.

The project was the Aquarian Nexus, a network designed to facilitate the free exchange of knowledge and resources among diverse planetary systems, promoting unity and cooperation on a cosmic scale. The Doctor, with their extensive experience across time and space, and Alex, with their deep understanding of astrological interconnectedness, were uniquely positioned to contribute to this endeavor.

Their task involved navigating the complex dynamics of interstellar diplomacy and technology, working to integrate the myriad systems into a cohesive whole. This required not just technical prowess but a profound understanding of the diverse cultures and societies that would be connected by the Nexus.

As they engaged with this challenge, the Doctor and Alex encountered various representatives from different worlds, each with their own perspectives and needs. Through these interactions, they learned the importance of listening and collaboration, realizing that true innovation arises not from the pursuit of individual glory but from the collective effort towards a common goal.

The completion of the Nexus was a moment of triumph, not just for the Doctor and Alex but for all who had contributed to its realization. It stood as a beacon of Aquarian ideals, a testament to the power of unity and innovation in fostering progress and harmony.

The Visionaries of Aquarius, in recognition of their contributions, bestowed upon them the Emblem of the Water-Bearer, symbolizing the flow of wisdom, creativity, and unity that they had helped to unleash. It was a reminder that the most profound changes often come from the pooling of collective efforts and the daring to dream of a better future.

With the wisdom of Aquarius illuminating their journey, the Doctor and Alex moved forward, their spirits buoyed by the experience of having contributed to something greater than themselves. They carried with them the lessons of innovation, community, and the understanding that progress is not the domain of the few but the shared destiny of all.

Their celestial odyssey was drawing to a close, but the insights gained in Aquarius would continue to inspire them, a beacon of hope for the adventures that lay ahead, guided by the ancient and enduring wisdom of the stars.

Pisces: The Voyage of Compassion and Connection

The journey through the zodiac constellations reached its culmination in the ethereal realm of Pisces. After the innovative energy of Aquarius, the world of Pisces offered a starkly different experience. This domain was an immersive, boundless ocean, a dreamscape where the boundaries between reality and imagination, self and other, were blurred. Pisces, a mutable water sign, is known for its depth of empathy, intuition, and the unifying thread of universal love that binds all beings. Here, the essence of Pisces was felt as a profound connection to all of existence, an infinite sea of compassion and understanding.

Upon entering this realm, the Doctor and Alex found themselves not just walking but floating, as if buoyed by the waters of cosmic empathy that flowed through Pisces. The landscape around them shimmered with iridescent light, each wave and ripple a melody of emotions and dreams shared by every conscious being.

They were greeted by the Guardians of the Deep, ethereal beings who embodied the highest ideals of Pisces. The Guardians welcomed them with a warmth that felt like a homecoming, a reminder of the interconnectedness of all life. The challenge in Pisces was to undertake a voyage across the Celestial Sea, a journey that would require them to navigate the depths of their own souls and the collective unconscious of the universe.

The Celestial Sea was a mirror of the vast spectrum of experiences and emotions that define the sentient journey. Along the way, the Doctor and Alex encountered various souls adrift in the waters, each representing different facets of the human condition—joy and sorrow, fear and hope, isolation and connection. With the TARDIS as their vessel, they navigated these waters, extending a hand of compassion and understanding to those they met, weaving a tapestry of empathy that bridged the distance between disparate hearts and minds.

The voyage was as much an inward journey as it was an outward one. The Doctor, with their timeless wisdom, and Alex, with their empathetic heart, delved into their own depths, confronting their fears and desires, and in doing so, discovered the boundless compassion that lies within. This journey through Pisces taught them that true strength lies in vulnerability, that healing comes from the acknowledgment of one's own pain and the pain of others, and that the greatest power is found in the act of unconditional love.

As their journey reached its end, the Guardians of the Deep bestowed upon them the Piscean Crystal, a luminescent stone that pulsed with the light of a thousand stars, a symbol of the eternal bond that connects all beings. It was a reminder that in the vastness of the universe, no one is ever truly alone, and that the light of compassion can illuminate the darkest depths.

With the wisdom of Pisces guiding them, the Doctor and Alex emerged from the realm transformed, their hearts open and their spirits enriched by the profound connections they had forged. As they bid farewell to the zodiac constellations, they carried with them the lessons of empathy, compassion, and the understanding that the journey of the soul is an endless ocean, where every drop is a part of the whole, and every wave a story of connection and love.

Their celestial odyssey had come to an end, but the insights and experiences gained from each constellation would continue to guide them as they navigated the uncharted territories of the universe, their spirits forever marked by the ancient wisdom of the stars.

Chapter 3: Mercury Retrograde

After the enlightening journey through the zodiac constellations, the Doctor and Alex found themselves thrust into a new challenge, one that would test their resilience and understanding of cosmic forces in a way they hadn't anticipated. As they navigated the vastness of space, the TARDIS began to exhibit unusual symptoms: screens flickered without reason, the familiar hum of the engine stuttered, and communication devices refused to function properly. The Doctor, with a look of concern mixed with curiosity, quickly deduced the cause—a phenomenon dreaded by travelers of both space and time: Mercury retrograde.

Mercury retrograde, in astrological terms, is a period when the planet Mercury appears to move backward in its orbit from the perspective of Earth. It is a time associated with confusion, delay, and miscommunication, where the flow of information is disrupted, and technology often fails to cooperate. For the Doctor and Alex, this meant dealing with a cascade of minor mishaps that threatened to become a major crisis.

Determined to find a solution, the Doctor navigated the TARDIS to a nearby space station, hoping to find the tools and resources needed to correct the temporal disarray. However, upon arrival, they discovered that the space station was caught in a temporal anomaly of its own: time flowed backward, encapsulating the chaos and confusion of Mercury retrograde in a literal sense.

The space station, once a bustling hub of intergalactic trade and communication, was now a maze of contradictions, where greetings were goodbyes and the future was more familiar than the past. The inhabitants, trapped in this reverse temporality, struggled to make sense of their existence, their lives unraveling in reverse as they sought to understand what had happened.

The Doctor and Alex, unaffected by the time anomaly due to the TARDIS's protective mechanisms, set out to understand the astrological implications of Mercury and how they might fix the time anomaly.

They delved into ancient texts and astrological charts, seeking clues in the alignment of the planets and the historical significance of Mercury retrograde periods.

Through their research, they uncovered that the space station was located at a focal point of cosmic energy, a place where the influences of Mercury were magnified. The retrograde motion of Mercury, combined with the station's unique position in space, had created a vortex of temporal energy that reversed the flow of time. To correct this, they would need to realign the station's temporal field with the natural flow of time, essentially 'flipping' the energy vortex to restore normality.

The solution lay in a combination of astrological knowledge and temporal mechanics. The Doctor devised a plan to use the TARDIS's engines to generate a counter-vortex, while Alex calculated the precise astrological alignments needed to anchor the station in the correct temporal flow. It was a delicate operation, requiring precise timing and coordination, as well as a deep understanding of the symbiotic relationship between celestial movements and the fabric of time itself.

As they initiated the procedure, the chaos of Mercury retrograde intensified around them. Communications equipment sparked to life, only to spout nonsensical messages; tools behaved unpredictably, and the very walls of the space station seemed to flicker and warp. Yet, amidst the pandemonium, the Doctor and Alex remained focused, their actions guided by a blend of science and astrology that transcended the chaos.

Finally, with a burst of light and a resounding thrum, the counter-vortex stabilized, and time snapped back into its proper flow. The space station, once trapped in reverse, resumed its place in the forward march of time, its inhabitants blinking in confusion before gradually realizing that they were free from the anomaly.

In the aftermath, the Doctor and Alex reflected on the adventure, recognizing the power of Mercury retrograde not just to disrupt but to teach. They had faced the chaos of miscommunication and technological mishaps, only to emerge with a deeper understanding of the universe's intricate balance. The space station, restored to normality, served as a reminder that even in the face of cosmic confusion, knowledge, and perseverance could restore harmony.

As they set off from the space station, the TARDIS crew carried with them the lessons of Mercury retrograde, prepared to face the universe's next challenge with a renewed sense of purpose and the wisdom of the stars to guide them.

Chapter 4: The Moon's Illusion

After navigating the tumultuous waves of Mercury retrograde, the Doctor and Alex found their next destination to be seemingly tranquil in comparison: a distant moon bathed in a soft, silver glow. This celestial body, however, was no ordinary satellite; it was renowned across the cosmos for its potent influence on emotions and perceptions, a direct reflection of the Moon's astrological traits of intuition, emotional depth, and the unconscious.

Upon setting foot on the moon's surface, which shimmered with an ethereal light, the Doctor and Alex immediately sensed a shift in their own emotional states. The atmosphere was thick with a palpable, psychic energy that seemed to amplify feelings, memories, and desires, casting an illusionary veil over reality. The Doctor, familiar with the lore of countless worlds, recognized this as the work of the Moon's Illusion, a phenomenon where the moon's energies manifest the innermost thoughts and fears of those who traverse its lands.

Determined to understand the source of this powerful energy and hoping to harness it for good, the Doctor and Alex embarked on a journey across the moon's surface. The landscape around them was ever-changing, morphing in response to their subconscious minds, creating a labyrinth of memories and fantasies that were difficult to distinguish from reality.

As they ventured deeper into the heart of the illusion, the Doctor and Alex were confronted by manifestations of their deepest fears and desires. For the Doctor, this meant facing echoes of past losses and the weight of centuries of solitude; for Alex, it was the struggle with self-doubt and the longing for a place to truly belong. These apparitions, though intangible, were intensely real to them, forcing them to confront aspects of themselves they had long avoided.

The journey through the Moon's Illusion became a quest for inner understanding. The Doctor and Alex realized that to navigate this emotional landscape, they needed to rely not on logic or reason but on intuition and emotional balance. They began to embrace the moon's energy, using it to enhance their emotional awareness and to see through the illusions that had ensnared them.

Through this process, they discovered that the moon's power did not lie in creating illusions but in revealing truths—truths about their fears, desires, and the unresolved emotions that shaped their journeys. By confronting these aspects of themselves, the Doctor and Alex found a new level of understanding and acceptance, recognizing that emotional depth and intuition were as crucial to their survival as intellect and courage.

The climax of their adventure came when they reached the heart of the moon, where the energy was most potent. Here, they found an ancient obelisk, pulsating with the moon's power, serving as the nexus of the emotional energies that enveloped the moon. By acknowledging and accepting their deepest emotions in the presence of the obelisk, the Doctor and Alex were able to dissipate the illusions, calming the moon's turbulent energy.

As the illusions faded, the Doctor and Alex were left in a landscape of serene beauty, the moon now reflecting not their fears, but the peace that comes with emotional clarity and balance. The experience taught them the importance of embracing their emotions, not as weaknesses but as strengths, and the value of intuition in guiding them through the unknown.

With the Moon's Illusion resolved, the Doctor and Alex continued their journey, their bond strengthened and their spirits lifted by the knowledge that emotional insight and intuition were powerful tools in navigating the cosmos. They had learned that the greatest challenges often lie within and that facing them with courage and openness could lead to profound growth and understanding.

Chapter 5: The Solar Flare

After the emotional odyssey on the moon, the TARDIS set its course closer to the heart of the solar system, where the Sun, in all its blazing glory, dominated the heavens. This journey was not just a voyage through space but also a dive into the ancient and powerful astrological significance of the Sun itself. The Sun, in astrology, is considered the core of one's identity, representing the ego, the self, and the spirit. It influences personality traits, vitality, and the essence of individuality.

As the TARDIS navigated the intense solar winds and magnetic fields, the Doctor and Alex arrived at a vibrant planet orbiting close to the Sun. This world was home to the Helions, a civilization that revered the Sun as the ultimate source of astrological power and life. The Helions had built their society around the study of solar movements and their astrological implications, believing that the Sun's cycles and flares were direct messages from the divine.

Upon their arrival, the Doctor and Alex were welcomed with open arms, as the Helions were in the midst of a crisis. Their astrologers had predicted an imminent catastrophic solar flare, one so powerful that it threatened to engulf their planet and obliterate all forms of life. This prediction had thrown the Helions into a state of despair, for while they worshiped the Sun, they also respected its destructive power.

The Doctor, with a keen understanding of both celestial mechanics and the cultural significance of astrology, offered to help. Together with Alex, they began to work closely with the Helion astrologers, combining scientific knowledge with astrological wisdom to devise a plan to avert the disaster.

During their time with the Helions, the Doctor and Alex engaged in deep discussions about the influence of the Sun sign in astrology and how it shapes personality. The Helions believed that the position of the Sun at the moment of an individual's birth bestowed certain qualities and potential upon them. This belief mirrored many of the Doctor and Alex's encounters across the cosmos, where personality traits often aligned with the astrological readings of the Sun sign.

The Doctor explained how the Sun's gravitational pull and magnetic fields influenced not just planets but the very fabric of space-time. They theorized that by understanding these forces, they could predict the solar flare's path and devise a shield to protect the planet. This approach required a delicate balance of science and astrology, acknowledging the Sun's physical power and its symbolic significance.

Working tirelessly, the Doctor, Alex, and the Helion astrologers constructed a device capable of harnessing the TARDIS's energy to create a protective field around the planet. This field would not only deflect the solar flare but also channel some of its energy to the planet's power grid, turning a potentially catastrophic event into a source of strength.

As the solar flare approached, the Helions gathered, their eyes fixed on the sky, and their hearts filled with hope. When it finally erupted, the flare was indeed magnificent, a torrent of pure solar energy that would have been devastating if not for the intervention of the Doctor and Alex. The protective field activated, enveloping the planet in a shimmering aura that reflected the flare's energy away while absorbing its power.

In the aftermath, the Helions celebrated, their faith in the Sun as a source of life and destruction reaffirmed, but now tempered with the knowledge that science and astrology could work hand in hand to protect and enrich their civilization. The Doctor and Alex were honored as heroes, their names forever etched in the annals of Helion history.

As they departed, the Doctor and Alex reflected on the significance of the Sun in astrology and in life. They had seen firsthand how the essence of one's Sun sign could influence personality and destiny, and how the physical power of the Sun itself could shape the fate of civilizations. The journey to the Sun had been a testament to the interplay between cosmic forces and human belief, a reminder that the universe was a place of wonder, where science and spirituality could coexist in harmony.

Chapter 6: Venusian Harmony

Following their sun-drenched adventures, the Doctor and Alex set their sights on Venus, intrigued by reports of unexplained phenomena intricately linked to themes of love and relationships. Venus, in astrology, governs love, beauty, harmony, and the arts, along with the principles of attraction, pleasure, and emotional connection. These qualities were about to become central to their experiences on the planet that shared its name with the Roman goddess of love.

As the TARDIS materialized on Venus, they were greeted by a world of breathtaking beauty. The landscape was a riot of colors, with flora and fauna that seemed to thrive in the planet's thick, cloud-covered environment. The air was perfumed with an intoxicating blend of scents, and the very atmosphere seemed to thrum with the energy of harmony and attraction. The Venusians, a people who embodied the quintessence of their planet's astrological significance, welcomed the Doctor and Alex with open arms, eager to share their culture and seek help with the mysterious disturbances that threatened their way of life.

The unexplained phenomena had begun as small, isolated incidents: artworks losing their color, gardens wilting without cause, and, most alarmingly, a growing sense of discord among partners and communities. These events were antithetical to everything Venus stood for, and the Venusians were at a loss, their usual diplomatic and harmonious methods failing to resolve the escalating crisis.

Delving into the mystery, the Doctor and Alex quickly realized that the disturbances were not random but symptomatic of a deeper imbalance within the planet's core energies. Venus, so long a beacon of harmony and love, was suffering from a kind of spiritual malaise, a disconnect from the principles that had guided its inhabitants for millennia.

Exploring Venusian culture further, they discovered that the planet's arts, its methods of communication, and even its governance were all deeply intertwined with the qualities of Venus in astrology. Music, poetry, and visual arts were not mere pastimes but vital aspects of Venusian life, each reflecting the beauty and harmony that facilitated their peaceful existence. Diplomacy was prized over conflict, and relationships, in all forms, were considered sacred bonds.

The key to resolving the conflict, the Doctor hypothesized, lay in restoring Venus's connection to its core qualities. They suggested a grand convocation of the Venusians, a gathering that would combine the planet's artistic, diplomatic, and communal strengths. Through a ceremony that celebrated Venusian culture's depth and richness, they would rekindle the populace's connection to their planet's astrological essence.

The convocation was a spectacle of beauty and harmony, with music that resonated in the soul, art that captured the eye and the imagination, and words that healed and brought together. Alex, moved by the display, contributed with a heartfelt speech that drew upon their journey through the cosmos, highlighting the universal themes of love and connection that bound all beings. The Doctor, meanwhile, worked to amplify the ceremony's effects, subtly adjusting the TARDIS's energy to resonate with Venus's core, reinforcing the planet's natural vibrations of love and harmony.

As the ceremony reached its climax, a visible change swept over Venus. The colors of the artworks deepened, the gardens burst into vibrant life, and a sense of peace and joy suffused the air. The Venusians, their spirits lifted and their bonds renewed, felt the discord and malaise lift, replaced by a renewed sense of purpose and unity.

In the aftermath of the convocation, the Venusians celebrated not just the restoration of their culture and relationships but also the deeper understanding of their connection to Venus's astrological influences. They thanked the Doctor and Alex, now honored guests, for reminding them of the power of love, beauty, and diplomacy to overcome even the most perplexing challenges.

As the Doctor and Alex departed Venus, they reflected on the profound impact of astrological forces on the lives and societies they encountered. Venusian Harmony had been more than an adventure; it had been a lesson in the power of love and the essential need for balance and harmony in the universe. They left behind a world rejuvenated, a testament to the enduring strength of the qualities governed by Venus, ready to face the next chapter of their cosmic journey with hearts full and spirits uplifted.

Chapter 7: The Outer Planets

Embarking from the harmonious world of Venus, the Doctor and Alex set their course for the outer planets, each a realm of vast power and deep astrological significance. Their journey through these celestial giants—Jupiter, Saturn, Uranus, Neptune, and Pluto—promised not only thrilling adventures but profound lessons in growth, structure, revolution, illusion, and transformation.

Jupiter: The Realm of Growth and Expansion

Their first destination was Jupiter, a planet synonymous with growth, expansion, and the benevolent qualities of luck and prosperity in astrological lore. As they navigated the swirling clouds and monumental storms of the gas giant, they encountered the Jovians, a race of beings whose society was built on the principles of expansion and exploration.

However, a crisis loomed over Jupiter's horizon. A massive storm, larger and more destructive than any seen before, threatened to engulf Jovian settlements, a stark reminder of the planet's overwhelming power to both give and take away. The Doctor and Alex, drawing on Jupiter's astrological essence, inspired the Jovians to harness their collective resources and knowledge, expanding their technological capabilities to avert the disaster. This experience taught them the importance of growth, not just outwardly but inwardly, turning challenges into opportunities for advancement.

Saturn: The World of Structure and Karma

Next, they ventured to Saturn, a planet revered and feared for its associations with structure, discipline, and karma. Saturn challenged them with its rings of ice and rock, symbolic barriers that tested their resolve and commitment. The Saturnians, a people who lived by strict codes and laws, faced a societal upheaval that threatened to dissolve the very structures that defined them.

The Doctor and Alex, understanding Saturn's lessons of responsibility and endurance, guided the Saturnians to see beyond their rigid frameworks, finding balance between order and flexibility. By embracing Saturn's karmic lessons, they helped rebuild a society that valued structure but was also resilient and adaptable, a true testament to the planet's teachings on the necessity of solid foundations tempered by the wisdom of experience.

Uranus: The Sphere of Revolution and Change

Uranus beckoned with its promise of revolution and change, a planet where the unexpected was the only expectation. Here, the Doctor and Alex found themselves amidst a cultural renaissance, a breaking away from old traditions to explore new ways of thinking and being. The Uranians, vibrant and eccentric, were at the forefront of astronomical advancements, their society a living embodiment of Uranus's astrological inclination towards innovation and freedom.

However, with great change came conflict and chaos. The Doctor and Alex navigated the tumult, using Uranus's disruptive energy to fuel a movement towards a more inclusive and diverse future. They learned that true progress often comes from the courage to break away from the past and embrace the new, a lesson that resonated deeply with both travelers.

Neptune: The Domain of Illusion and Enlightenment

Neptune's mysterious and elusive nature was next, a planet where reality blended with dreams, and truths were hidden within illusions. Here, the Doctor and Alex embarked on a quest for enlightenment, delving into the depths of Neptune's oceans to uncover ancient wisdom lost to time. The Neptunians, ethereal and intuitive, struggled to discern reality from the illusions that shrouded their planet.

By confronting and understanding their own illusions, the Doctor and Alex led the Neptunians to a collective awakening, revealing the enlightenment that lies beyond deception. Neptune's lesson was clear: true understanding and insight often require navigating through layers of illusion, a journey that demands intuition and faith in one's inner vision.

Pluto: The Realm of Transformation and Power

Finally, they arrived at Pluto, a dwarf planet whose astrological significance belies its size, associated with transformation, power, and the cycle of death and rebirth. Pluto presented the most profound challenge: facing the shadows and the depths of the subconscious. The Plutonians, resilient and introspective, found themselves on the brink of a societal rebirth, a transformation that required letting go of old identities to embrace a new era.

The Doctor and Alex, through trials that tested their strength and resolve, helped the Plutonians navigate this period of intense change. Together, they unearthed ancient secrets that held the key to Pluto's transformative power, facilitating a rebirth that was both an end and a beginning. In Pluto's dark, icy realms, they learned that true power comes from the courage to confront the deepest parts of oneself and the world, embracing change as the pathway to new life.

Conclusion

As the TARDIS departed Pluto, the Doctor and Alex reflected on the odyssey through the outer planets. Each world had presented unique challenges and lessons that, when woven together, formed a tapestry of astrological wisdom spanning growth and expansion, structure and karma, revolution and change, illusion and enlightenment, and transformation and power. These adventures deepened their understanding of the universe's complexities and the intricate dance between cosmic forces and individual destiny, forever shaping their journey through the stars.

Chapter 8: The Alignment

After their profound journey through the outer planets, the Doctor and Alex were drawn back to the mystery that had initiated their cosmic odyssey: the cryptic signals resembling astrological symbols. With a deeper understanding of astrological lore and its impact on various civilizations, they were now ready to unravel the final piece of the puzzle.

The mysterious signals, they discovered, were not mere calls for help but a prophecy predicting a rare and catastrophic astrological alignment. This alignment, involving all the planets they had visited, threatened to disrupt the fabric of the universe itself. The gravitational and magical forces generated by this alignment could tear apart the delicate balance between the physical and etherial, leading to chaos on a cosmic scale.

Faced with this daunting challenge, the Doctor and Alex understood that preventing the catastrophe would require more than their knowledge and skills alone. It demanded a convergence of beings from across the solar system, each bringing their unique perspectives and abilities to create a unified force strong enough to counter the threat.

The Doctor reached out to the civilizations they had encountered: the expansive Jovians, disciplined Saturnians, revolutionary Uranians, enlightened Neptunians, and transformative Plutonians, along with representatives from Venus, Mars, and Mercury. Each had experienced firsthand the lessons of their ruling planets and understood the stakes involved.

As these diverse beings gathered, a council was formed, symbolizing the unity and interconnectedness of all things. The Doctor, with Alex by their side, explained the nature of the alignment and the potential for universal unravelling. The air was tense with the weight of the impending disaster, but also alive with the potential of collective action.

The plan was as audacious as it was necessary: to use the unique energies and qualities of each planet, amplified and directed by the united will and technology of the assembled representatives, to create a counter-alignment. This counter-alignment would not only neutralize the disruptive forces but also weave a stronger, more harmonious fabric of cosmic energy, reinforcing the unity between the physical and astrological realms.

The execution of the plan required precise timing, coordination, and the willingness to share and blend the diverse powers and knowledge each civilization brought to the table. The Doctor and Alex, acting as conduits and mediators, facilitated this monumental effort, guiding the collective energies towards the focal point of the disruption.

As the moment of the alignment approached, the assembled beings focused their intentions, channeling the essence of their planets through a matrix of technology and magic, ancient runes and advanced algorithms, all converging on the TARDIS, which acted as the nexus for their efforts.

The alignment began, stars and planets moving into the prophesied configuration, the universe holding its breath as the forces of unraveling met the shield of united will and energy. For a moment, the tension was unbearable, the outcome uncertain. Then, slowly, the disruptive energies began to dissipate, absorbed and neutralized by the counter-alignment, the fabric of the universe not only mended but strengthened by the unprecedented unity of its defenders.

In the aftermath, the representatives from each planet stood together, a testament to what could be achieved through cooperation and understanding. The Doctor and Alex looked on, their hearts full, knowing that they had not only averted a catastrophe but also fostered a new level of cosmic collaboration.

The mysterious signals, once a harbinger of doom, had become a symbol of hope, a call to unity that had been answered by the diverse inhabitants of the solar system. The Doctor mused on the beauty of the universe's complexity, its challenges, and its wonders, all interconnected in the vast dance of existence.

As the TARDIS set off once more, the Doctor and Alex carried with them the lessons of The Alignment: that in the vast, intricate tapestry of the cosmos, every thread is essential, every pattern meaningful, and the strength of the whole lies in the unity of its parts. The universe, in all its diversity and mystery, was a little bit safer, a little bit closer, thanks to their efforts and the unprecedented alliance they had forged.

Chapter 9: The Eclipse

In the aftermath of the grand alignment, the universe settled into a fragile peace. However, the cosmos had one final trial for the Doctor and Alex, a challenge that would mark both an end and a beginning: a solar eclipse that would cast its shadow not just across the Earth, but through the very fabric of time and space.

The eclipse was no ordinary celestial event but a convergence of cosmic forces, amplified by the recent alignment. It threatened to undo the harmony the Doctor and Alex had fought so hard to achieve. With the shadow of the moon poised to obscure the Sun's light, a symbolic darkness loomed, one that held the power to plunge the universe into chaos unless the Doctor and Alex could muster all they had learned on their journey to realign the planets once more.

This time, the challenge was not just external but deeply personal. The eclipse, acting as a mirror to the soul, brought unexpected revelations. For the Doctor, it unearthed long-buried memories and desires, casting light on the shadowy corners of their timeless existence. For Alex, it was a moment of profound transformation, an opportunity to step beyond the role of companion and into a destiny that had been quietly shaping since their journey began.

As the eclipse approached, the Doctor and Alex raced against time, weaving through the tapestry of the cosmos with the TARDIS, drawing upon every scrap of knowledge and experience they had gained. They revisited the planets of the outer solar system, gathering energy signatures, ancient artifacts, and the goodwill of the civilizations they had aided.

The battle against chaos was not fought with weapons but with willpower, wisdom, and the collective hopes of countless beings. As the eclipse began, casting its shadow over planet after planet, the Doctor and Alex initiated the realignment. Using the TARDIS as a conduit, they channeled the combined energies of the solar system, focusing them into a beam of pure intention aimed at the heart of the eclipse.

The moment of totality was a breathless, timeless pause, a dance of light and shadow that held the fate of the universe in its balance. Then, slowly, the shadow began to recede, the Sun's light breaking through in a radiant corona that bathed the cosmos in warmth and brilliance. The chaos that lurked at the edge of existence was held at bay, the harmony of the universe restored by the hands of those who had traversed its wonders and terrors.

But the true victory lay in the transformations wrought by the eclipse. The Doctor emerged from the trial with a renewed sense of purpose, their bond with the universe and its myriad lives deepened by the challenges they had faced. Alex, transformed by the journey and the revelations of the eclipse, stepped into a new role, no longer just a traveler but a guardian of the cosmos in their own right.

In the quiet aftermath of the eclipse, as the universe settled into a new equilibrium, the Doctor and Alex shared a moment of reflection. They had witnessed the end of one cycle and the beginning of another, a reminder that in the cosmic dance of light and shadow, destruction and creation, there is always renewal, always hope.

The eclipse, with its profound darkness and resplendent light, was a symbol of the endless cycle of endings and beginnings that defines the universe and those who journey through it. For the Doctor and Alex, it was both a farewell to the path they had walked together and the dawn of new adventures, new challenges, and new transformations.

As the TARDIS disappeared into the vortex, its destination unknown, the legacy of their journey remained—a testament to the power of unity, the resilience of the spirit, and the endless wonder of the cosmos. The eclipse was not an ending but a promise, a gateway to infinite possibilities, and the enduring light that shines through the darkest of shadows.

Conclusion: The Astrological Key

As the cosmic dance of the eclipse faded into the tapestry of the universe, the Doctor and Alex found themselves once more amidst the quiet hum of the TARDIS, its ancient walls echoing with the memories of their journey. Surrounded by the vastness of space and time, they reflected on the adventures that had unfolded, the mysteries unraveled, and the transformations experienced. It was a moment of profound contemplation, not just of their own paths but of the universe's intricate designs.

Throughout their odyssey across the solar system, astrology had served as a guide, a challenge, and a revelation. It had opened their eyes to the deep connections between the celestial bodies and the narrative of existence. The Doctor, with countless years and countless journeys behind them, marveled at how astrology had woven its way through their travels, often unnoticed but always there, influencing, guiding, and illuminating.

Alex, whose journey with the Doctor had been a voyage of discovery not just of the universe but of the self, realized that astrology had offered them a lens through which to view the cosmos in a new light. It was a key that unlocked the mysteries of time and space, revealing the cosmic dance of energies and forces that shaped destinies and forged connections across the vast expanse of existence.

Together, they acknowledged that astrology, with its deep connection to time and space, had always been a part of their travels, an underlying current that pulsed with the rhythm of the universe itself.

It was a reminder that the cosmos was not just a place of physical laws and random chaos but a living, breathing entity, imbued with meaning, purpose, and a profound interconnectedness.

The journey through the zodiac constellations and the challenges of the planets had taught them invaluable lessons about harmony, balance, growth, and transformation. These lessons were not just astrological principles but universal truths, guiding lights for navigating the complexities of existence. The Doctor and Alex came to see astrology not as a mere system of divination but as a language of the cosmos, a way to understand the subtle nuances and profound connections that bound all things.

As they set their sights on new horizons, the Doctor and Alex felt a renewed sense of wonder and curiosity. The universe was vast, filled with endless mysteries and boundless opportunities for adventure. They pondered the possibility of exploring other mystical and mythological systems, each with its own keys to unlocking the secrets of the cosmos. From the runic alphabets of ancient Earth to the celestial mythologies of distant worlds, countless adventures awaited, each promising new insights and new challenges.

The journey through the astrological realms had been but one chapter in their endless voyage across time and space. As they prepared to embark on the next chapter, the Doctor and Alex knew that the astrological key would remain with them, a symbol of their journey and a reminder of the deep, cosmic connection that underpinned their travels.

The TARDIS, timeless and ever-ready, hummed to life, its engines echoing with the promise of future adventures. Wherever they went, whatever mysteries they sought to unravel, the Doctor and Alex would carry with them the wisdom of the stars, guided by the ancient and enduring light of astrology.

And so, with the universe stretching out before them, full of mysteries to solve and tales to tell, the Doctor and Alex stepped into the unknown, their spirits alight with the endless possibilities of adventure, their hearts open to the infinite wonders of the cosmos. The journey continues, and with it, the endless dance of light and shadow, of stars and destinies intertwined.

Epilogue: A New Dawn

As the echoes of their latest adventure faded into the endless expanse of space, the Doctor and their companion found themselves bathed in the soft glow of the TARDIS console room, the familiar hum of the time machine a comforting melody in the silence that followed. The universe was safe, at least for now, but the journey they had undertaken had left an indelible mark on both traveler and companion.

For the Doctor, whose long life had been filled with countless adventures and extraordinary encounters, the recent odyssey had been a reminder of the profound interconnectedness of all things. They had witnessed the power of unity, the resilience of the spirit, and the enduring light that shines through the darkest of shadows. It was a lesson that would stay with them, guiding their actions and shaping their destiny as they continued their journey through time and space.

As for their companion, who had joined the Doctor on a path of discovery and wonder, the adventure had been a journey of self-discovery and transformation. They had faced challenges, confronted fears, and emerged stronger and wiser for the experience. The mysteries of the universe had opened their eyes to the vastness of possibility, and they had embraced the cosmic dance with a newfound sense of purpose and wonder.

Together, the Doctor and their companion stood on the threshold of a new dawn, ready to continue their exploration of the cosmos armed with a deeper understanding of its astrological dimensions. The stars beckoned, their light casting a path through the darkness of the unknown, inviting the travelers to chart new courses, encounter new civilizations, and unravel new mysteries that lay hidden among the galaxies.

But even as they embarked on their next adventure, the Doctor and their companion knew that the cosmos was vast and full of mysteries beyond imagining. The universe would always be a place of wonder and awe, an endless expanse of possibility waiting to be explored. And as they journeyed forth into the unknown, they carried with them the spirit of adventure, the courage to face the unknown, and the boundless curiosity that had defined their lives.

In the end, the story of the Doctor and their companion was but one chapter in the infinite tapestry of existence, a fleeting moment in the grand scheme of time and space. But for those who dared to dream, who dared to imagine the wonders that awaited beyond the stars, the adventure would never truly end. For the universe was alive with possibility, and the journey was only just beginning.

<u>Message from the Author:</u>

I hope you enjoyed this book, I love astrology and knew there was not a book such as this out on the shelf. I love metaphysical items as well. Please check out my other books:

-Life of Government Benefits

-My life of Hell

-My life with Hydrocephalus

-Red Sky

-World Domination:Woman's rule

-World Domination:Woman's Rule 2: The War

-Life and Banishment of Apophis: book 1

-The Kidney Friendly Diet

-The Ultimate Hemp Cookbook

-Creating a Dispensary(legally)

-Cleanliness throughout life: the importance of showering from childhood to adulthood.

-Strong Roots: The Risks of Overcoddling children

-Hemp Horoscopes: Cosmic Insights and Earthly Healing

- Celestial Hemp Navigating the Zodiac: Through the Green Cosmos

-Astrological Hemp: Aligning The Stars with Earth's Ancient Herb

-The Astrological Guide to Hemp: Stars, Signs, and Sacred Leaves

-Green Growth: Innovative Marketing Strategies for your Hemp Products and Dispensary

-Cosmic Cannabis

-Astrological Munchies

-Henry The Hemp

-Zodiacal Roots: The Astrological Soul Of Hemp

- **Green Constellations: Intersection of Hemp and Zodiac**

-Hemp in The Houses: An astrological Adventure Through The Cannabis Galaxy

-Galactic Ganja Guide

Heavenly Hemp

-Zodiac Leaves

Check out my Virtual dispensary for all your hemp needs: https://shift.store/sg1fan23477/retail

If you want solar for your home go here: https://www.harborsolar.live/apophisenterprises/

Instagrams: @apophis_enterprises, @hempkingdom2024, @apophisbookemporium, @apophisfashion, @apophisscardshop

Twitter: @apophisenterpr1, Tiktok:@apophisenterprise

Youtube: @sg1fan23477

Podcast: Apophis Chat Zone: https://open.spotify.com/show/5zXbrCLEV2xzCp8ybrfHsk?si=fb4d4fdbdce44dec

Newsletter: https://apophiss-newsletter-27c897.beehiiv.com/

www.ingramcontent.com/pod-product-compliance
Lightning Source LLC
Chambersburg PA
CBHW010939140726
47988CB00010B/3525